THE EGYPTIAN MAU CAT

Didier HALLÉPÉE

Collection Animaux

THE EGYPTIAN MAU CAT

La loi du 11 mars 1957 n'autorisant, aux termes des alinéas 2 et 3 de l'article 41, d'une part, que les « copies ou reproductions strictement réservées à l'usage privé du copiste et non destinées à une utilisation collective » et d'autre part, que les analyses et les courtes citations dans un but d'exemple et d'illustration, « toute représentation ou reproduction intégrale, ou partielle, faites sans le consentement de l'auteur ou de ses ayants droit ou ayants cause est illicite » (alinéa 1° de l'article 40). Cette reproduction ou représentation, par quelque procédé que ce soit, constituerait donc une contrefaçon sanctionnée par les articles 425 et suivants du code pénal.

This book is sold subject to the condition that it shall not, by the way of trade or otherwise, be lent, resold, hired out, or otherwise circulated without the publisher's prior consent in any form of binding or cover other than that in which it is published and without a similar condition including this condition being imposed on the subsequent purchaser and without limiting the rights under copyright reserved above, no part of this publication may be reproduced, stored in or reproduced into a retrieval system or transmitted in any form or by any means (electronic, mechanical, photocopying, recording or otherwise), without the prior permission of both the copyright owner and the above-mentioned publisher of this book.

Copyright Didier Hallépée
2011

Didier HALLÉPÉE

THE EGYPTIAN MAU CAT

Same author, Carrefour du Net publisher, paper books

"Le chat mau égyptien", 2009
"Citations et proverbes chats et chiens", 2009
"Mot à mau, les pensées du chat mau", 2010
"Pensées Royales Canines, les pensées du King Charles", 2010
"Les enfants du chat mau – histoire du chat de race", 2011
"Mon chat m'a dit, mon chien m'a dit", 2011

"L'univers de la monétique", 2009
"Le Sepa, l'espace des paiements en euro", 2009
"Qualité et sécurité informatique, les méthodes CMPI et CMSI", 2009
"La sécurité NFC", 2011
"La sécurité des systèmes embarqués", 2011

Same author, Carrefour du Net publisher, ebooks
"A ma fille", 2011
"Secrets de chat", 2011
"Secrets de chien", 2011
"Sudoku-neko volume 1", 2011
"Sudoku-neko volume 2", 2011
"Sudoku-neko volume 3", 2011
"Djambi, l'échiquier de Machiavel, *suivi du Sabacc*", 2011
"Le jeu de go", 2011
"Mon chat m'a conté", 2011
"Mon chien m'a conté", 2011
"Mon coq m'a conté", 2011
"Les secrets de Bastet, précis de génétique féline", 2011

Same author, Carrefour du Net publisher, in English
"The Egyptian Mau cat", 2011
"The Egyptian Mau children – story of the breed cat", 2011
"My cat told me, my dog told me", 2011
"Mau Mews (photo-comic)", 2011
"King Barks (photo-comic)", 2011
"Cat Secrets", 2011
"Dog Secrets", 2011
"Sudoku-neko volume 1", 2011
"Sudoku-neko volume 2", 2011
"Sudoku-neko volume 3", 2011
"CMPI, Managing and Mastering Computer Projects", 2009

Same author, Carrefour du Net publisher, in Italian
"I figli del gatto mau – storia del gatto di razza", 2011

*Meet the author on his forum 'Fondcombe writers'
http://forum.fondcombe.com*

to Isabelle, Leia and Jacen
with all my love.

to Chantal, Sandrine, Bernard, Zoran, Brigitte et Nicolas who supported me in the mau book project.

To all AIME members who share with me the Mau passion.

to Steve, Becky, Dot et Dot who were first to help the french Maus across the Atlantic.

to Dianick and Vasar, the origin of our first Maus.

to Rafat, the friend who helped me in the Mau quest in the pyramid country.

To all people who love Egyptian Maus or who love cats.

WELCOME TO THE MARVELLOUS WORLD OF THE EGYPTIAN MAU CAT

It is a pleasure to guide you to the heart of the wonderful world of Egyptian Mau.

His name being Mau, meaning light, he naturally brightens our days.

In our imaginary, cats and Egypt are inseparable. That raises lots of questions: did the cat come from Egypt? And only from Egypt? Is the Mau the authentic descendant of the cats of the Pharaohs? And what about the cat before Egypt?

To answer all your questions we will roam the cat world together before discovering the Egyptian Mau himself.

So, we will first explore the main species of this little feline called Cat.

Then, from prehistory to Egypt, from Egypt to the Middle-Ages and from the Middle-Ages to our days, we will follow his journey through ages and continents until he finally reached us and our part of the world.

And finally, we will discover together the brightest of them, the authentic cat of pharaohs: the Egyptian Mau. We'll see how he crossed the seas and oceans on his path from Egypt to Italy and the United States, Switzerland and France where he has by now been a source of joy to us over the last ten years.

THE ORIGINS OF THE CAT

The main species of cats

The cat is a member of the Felidae family, genus Felis. Felis cats include all small felines. The smallest of them are called cats. The main species of cats are:

- *Felis sylvestris*   European wild cat
- *Felis lybica*   African wild cat
- *Felis chaus*   jungle cat
- *Felis margarita*   sand cat
- *Felis bieti*   Chinese desert cat
- *Felis manul*   Pallas cat
- *Felis nigripes*   black-footed cat
- *Felis catus*   domestic cat

<u>Felis sylvestris, the European wild cat</u>

The European wildcat coat has a color ranging from brown to gray, with black patterns and a short tail adorned with black rings and ending in a black tip. Its eyes are brown. It weighs about 8 kilos.

It is found throughout continental Europe and even in the Caucasus, especially in France, Germany, Poland, and on the shores of the Mediterranean Sea.

It lives mainly in forests. It feeds mostly on small mammals, reptiles and birds, but is not averse to insects and fish.

It hunts mainly at night. Its hunting area covers about 250 hectares. Although it lives alone, the hunt can be a couple or family group affair depending on environmental conditions.

It lives away from inhabited areas. Its kittens are naturally wild, even in captivity.

The European subspecies of wild cat is named Felis sylvestris sylvestris. The Asian subspecies is known as Felis sylvestris ornata.

Felis lybica, the African wild cat

The African wild cat has a gray coat with tabby or spotted patterns of black or red color. The color of these patterns is less pronounced for subjects living in desert areas. The black color of her rear leg pads is one of its distinguishing features. Compared to the European wildcat, it has shorter hair, a longer tail and a slender stockier stature. Its eyes are golden.

It is found nearly everywhere on the African continent, in its forests as well as in its plains and mountains. It feeds on small mammals, reptiles and birds but adapts to insects in some areas.

It hunts mainly at night. Its hunting area covers about 500 hectares. Although it lives alone, the hunt can be a couple or family group affair depending on environmental conditions.

Unlike the European wildcat, it is often found near human habitats. When and if brought into human contact, her kittens can be domesticated.

The African wild cat is now considered a subspecies of the wildcat known as Felis sylvestris lybica.

Felis chaus, the jungle cat

The jungle cat is also named swamp lynx

It has a coat ranging in color from sand yellow to red fawn, or black in some areas. Its coat is almost without marking (sometimes some stripes on the legs). Its hair has stripes of different colors (ticking). The ears end in a black tuft. It weighs 8 to 15 pounds. The kittens have a striped marking that disappears when becoming adults.

The jungle cat is the most widespread cat species ~~of cat~~ in Asia, from Egypt to China. It feeds on small mammals, frogs, reptiles and insects. It can also eat small antelopes.

It hunts by day. Its large ears allow it to spot its prey easily despite dense vegetation. It is capable of jumping higher than 2 meters to catch birds. These exploits have inspired striking scenes of bird hunting reproduced on Egyptian bas-reliefs.

Felis margarita, the sand cat

The sand cat has a thick fur, ranging in color from sand yellow to gray, more colorful on the back, and with clear marking on its muzzle and chest. It has a characteristic red makeup extending from the corner of the eye to the middle of the chin. Black marking is present all over the body, especially on the limbs and tail which ends with a black tip. It has a broad face, large yellow eyes, large triangular ears placed low, without tuft and with black tips. Ears and whiskers are well developed, which enables it to detect its prey efficiently, even if hidden under the desert surface. Its thick fur allows it to maintain its natural moisture both during the hot day and against the cold of the night. Its pads are trimmed with fur, which protects it from contact with a burning ground and gives it more lift in the sand. Its legs are short and powerful. It can dig a shelter for protection from the searing afternoon heat. It weighs about 2.5 pounds.

It is found in desert areas of northern Africa and southwest Asia, and in rocky areas near these deserts. It was identified by General Margueritte during an expedition in the heart of the Sahara desert, hence its name.

It hunts at dusk and at night when the temperature of the desert becomes bearable. It feeds on rodents, but finds lizards, insects and hares an appreciable food supplement. It drinks little because its water needs are met by consuming its preys. Its urinary system is adapted to the desert and uses little water, allowing it to survive for long periods without drinking. Its territory is very large.

Felis bieti, the Chinese desert cat

Chinese desert cat has a fur of a a yellow-gray color. Her hips are marked with brown spots or stripes. His cheeks are decorated with brown markings. Its tail is long, with 3 or 4 concentric rings and black extremity. It weighs 6 to 8 kilos.

It is found in rocky steppes and mountain areas in Central Asia, Mongolia and the part of China bordering Tibet. Despite its name, it is not found in desert areas.

The lifestyle and dietary habits of this cat are little known.

Felis manul, the Pallas cat

The Pallas cat has a fur with brown-gray, yellow or blue long hair. The end of hair is white. Usually, its coat has no marking, except on the cheeks and tail. Its legs are short and stocky, adapted to climbing. It weighs from 3 to 8 kilos.

It is found in Central Asia, from Tibet to the Caspian. It lives in both wooded and rocky areas and can live up to 4000 meters hight.

It is named Pallas cat, after a German naturalist, Peter Pallas, who observed that the cat had 28 teeth whereas the other species had 30.

It hunts at night and feeds on small rodents.

Felis nigripes, the black-footed cat

Its name comes from the black color of his pads.

The black-footed cat has a fur whose color can be yellow, brown, dark brown or gray. It has large brown spots on its back, stripes on its shoulders, rings on its legs and tail whose extremity is black. Its pads are black and its name is due to the long tufts of black hair growing between its toes. These hairs protect it from the soil heat and also enable it to detect insects under the soil. It is the smallest of felines. It weighs about 2 kilos.

It is found in the steppes and savannas of southern Africa.

It takes shelter in burrows abandoned by other animals (including rabbits). Its use of termite nests earned it the nickname "Tiger of termites."

It hunts at any hour with a preference for the night hours. It eats insects, squirrels, birds, reptiles, and even herbs. Local legends sometimes depict it as a hunter of antelopes and giraffes.

Cat and prehistoy

The first small felines wandered through our forests about 65 million years ago. Around 12 million years ago there appeared the first wild cats, including felis manul and felis martelli. The felis martelli is probably the ancestor of the European wildcat, felis sylvestris. The felis martelli disappeared about 1 million years ago.

After the first glaciation (900,000 years ago) there appeared the European wildcat: felis sylvestris. He lived in the vast forests of Europe. During the second glaciation (around 600,000 years ago), the species spread in Asia and Africa. With climate change, feline populations were separated and evolved into different species: European wildcat, African wildcat, jungle cat, sand cat, Chinese desert cat, Pallas's cat, black-footed cat.

These species are different but share a common genetic pool enabling them to inter-breed.

The Egyptian origin

The African wild cat was first attracted close to human habitats by the presence of rodents, which he ate. This is evidenced in particular by the presence of cat bones at a site of in Jericho dating from 9,000 BC, at a site in Cyprus dating back to 9,000 BC and at a site of / at Harappa (Indus Valley) dating from 4,000 BC.

Thanks to the discoveries of Cyprus website (Shillourokambos burial) we know that the cat was domesticated at that time. His keeping company with humans probably dates from the beginnings of agriculture, cats have been attracted into the villages by the mice who ate the standing grain.

On the other hand, the absence of visible morphological changes (reduction in size and skull) shows that domestication of the cat came later.

The grain silo was invented in Egypt about 4,000 years ago as a means to fight against famine due to crop failure. Some argue that the biblical story of Joseph and Pharaoh has something to do with this invention. The word "silo" comes from Tarbernacle of Shiloh (a biblical figure who lived at the time of Pharaoh Shishak, 950-929 BC) that contained the seeds, which served as offerings (Exodus and Deuteronomy).

The silos attracted rodents then snakes. Thus the cat, who was already living near human dwellings, found so food in abundance and settled in the proximity of humans.

The usefulness of the cat was soon recognized and he was first bred for his predatory skills then domesticated. He then moved into the interior of houses and became a member of the family.

The Pharaoh himself acknowledged the usefulness of the cat and wanted to be the sole owner of members of the feline race. That's why the cat was erected as a semi-god, around 3,500 years ago. Thus, it could only belong to a god, Pharaoh himself. That is why even today in Egypt, the Maus are called Pharaonic cats.

Let's note that the rod of the Pharaoh ("heqa") has the elegant curve of the cat's tail.

So he was revered under the name of Bastet, a goddess who is sometimes represented as a cat, sometimes as a cat-headed woman holding a sitar in her right hand and wearing one or two gold rings.

Bubastis was chosen as the main place of worship of Bastet. The annual festivities in honor of Bastet, celebrated at Bubastis, attracted many pilgrims (which is attested by Herodotus). Bastet is still celebrated on October 31.

Bastet, known as the devouring goddess, represents at the same time fire, war, pestilence and disease, second home, fertility, sexuality and the protection of pregnant women and children. She is the wife and daughter of the god Ra. The cat's name in Egyptian is Mau and it refers both to the cat's mew and the light radiating from her. She is a two-look goddess: with her cat's head, it is Bastet, Lady of the East, associated with the moon (her son Khensu is the god of the moon); with the head of a lioness, she is Sekhmet, Queen of the West, combined with sunlight. She is also the goddess of pleasure, music, dance, joy. She is also Ra's instrument of vengeance. Her fits of rage are still famous.

The cult of Bastet reached its highest development around 950 BC. At that time, Bubastis became the capital of Egypt.

The love of the Egyptians for their cat was taken advantage of by the Persian king Cambyses II during his conquest of Egypt, during the siege of Pelusium (525 BC). According to legend, it took a lot of cats as hostage and made them stand in front of the shields of his soldiers. Rather than risk the lives of their cats, the Egyptians of Pelusium surrendered.

Grown into a divine animal, symbolizing fertility and fat years, the cat enjoyed all the benefits of his rank. Killing a cat, even accidentally, was a crime punishable by death. Diodorus relates (year 1 BC) that a Roman soldier killed a cat and nothing could prevent the mob in its fury from putting him to death, despite the risk of triggering a war with the Romans.

The Egyptians revered their cats and mourned their death. On the death of their cats, the Egyptians shaved their eyebrows in mourning. The dead cats were mummified and brought to the temple of Bastet at Bubastis. This practice was still in force in the early years of our era. The study of these mummies has revealed the young age of many of these cats and the presence of fractures at the neck: it seems that many cats were bred in the temples specifically to be mummified and sold as a charm for the home or as votive offerings: the offering of a mummified cat to Bastet unleashed the goddess's formidable rage against any enemy.

Hundreds of mummified cats could be found. Thus, scientists were able to identify these early cats as Felis lybica. Many mummies having preserved their fur, we know that they usually were yellow (bronze) and wore black spots or sometimes black stripes.

The cat was often depicted in bas-reliefs and papyruses. On these images, it is usually yellow or red. And adorned with spots or without marks. Hunting scenes let us suppose that he was trained to hunt birds.

The world conquest

The Egyptians considered their cats as precious property and as sacred animals. Therefore strict regulations prohibited their exportation.

Some of them were used very early on Egyptian ships exporting wheat.

The Phoenicians were the first to illegally export the cat, around 900 BC. Thus, they introduced it into Galilee, Greece, Italy.

Gradually, the domestic cat spreaded throughout Europe and the Middle East.

In Artashastra, a manual of Indian statecraft (IIIrd century BC), Kautilya describes how to use cats and mongooses against rats and snakes.

The story runs that Pope Gregory 1st (590-604) said during a sermon, "Give me one of your most expensive belongings as offering!" Hearing this, a monk came along and took a cat out from his sleeve to give it to him. The Pope smiled and in turn got a cat out of his own sleeve.

It was also said that the Prophet Muhammad (570-632) had been saved from a snake bite by a cat. He always carried Muessa, his pussy, inside the sleeve of his coat. One day, called for prayer, he had qualms about disturbing Muessa in his sleep. Then he cut off the sleeve to be able to go to prayer.

The cat's arrival in England is attested from the tenth century onwards but a cat was a rare sight at that time.

Around the tenth century, the city of Antwerp was burned because of a cat. A traveler had made a stopover in Antwerp, accompanied by his cat. Residents who had never seen a cat were conquered by his / its ability to catch rats and mice and therefore implored the traveler to give it to them (for gold). Hardly had the traveler departed than they ran after him to ask what the cat ate. "What it takes, you animals," he replied. The Antwerp people understood "what it takes, you *and* animals." They decided to get rid of it. Faced with the angry crowd, the cat sought refuge on the roof of a house. The crowd set fire to the house in order to kill this dangerous animal. Our cat escaped the fire by jumping onto the roof of the house next door. Gradually, much of the city of Antwerp was destroyed by fire without the cat being killed. Thus it was that the city of Antwerp was burned just because of a cat.

Very soon, the cat was associated with witchcraft. According to legend, the goddess of darkness, named Diane, loved Lucifer, who owned a cat. They had a daughter whom they sent down to earth along with Lucifer's cat to teach magic to humans. From the fifth century to the seventeenth century, the cat was considered by the Church as a pet animal of witches, and as such regularly burned. Thus it became much rarer throughout the Middle-Ages.

It was between the thirteenth century and the sixteenth centuries that the fight against the pagan cults and against cats was at its most intense. Lucifer being supposed to become incarnate as a black cat, the mere possession of a black cat was often evidence of witchcraft and led to the master and his cat being burned at the stake. That's why it is said that black cats bring bad luck. In contrast, the white cat symbolizes purity. In 1233, Pope Gregory IX launched the anathema on black cats and their owners. The animal's life could be spared, however, if he wore around his neck a white spot called "finger of God" or "mark of the angel."

Witches were reputed to be able to become incarnate nine times in the body of their cats. Hence the belief that the cat has nine lives.

When the great epidemics of plague decimated the population, the usefulness of the cat was again recognized. A papal edict allowed the convents of nuns to own a cat during plague epidemics ~~of plague~~.

The arrival of the Turkish Angora ended this ostracism, in the eighteenth century. The popularity of this cat with the European nobility was very large: an Angora cat was considered a royal gift. Suddenly, the common cat was back in favour as a household companion and a rodent hunter.

It was during the nineteenth century that the recognition of cat breeds first began, with the arrival of breeds from the East, the breeding and selection of cats and cat shows.

The cat accompanied sailors on their travels around the world and peopled the new settlements at the same time as man. On Clipperton Island, they proliferated so much that they nearly destroyed local wildlife and had to be exterminated.

Cats followed Europeans in their work of colonization. Thus our household cats returned to Egypt to enrich the gene pool of cats in ~~Egypt~~ that country and to interbreed with the direct descendants of the cats of Pharaoh.

The Asian and the Siberian origin

The Asian origin

The cat's presence in China appears to date back over 6,000 years. Domestication probably dates to the Han Dynasty (100 BC). The cat had already become common in China around 500 BC and in India around 200 BC. The first cat that arrived in Japan was as a gift from the Emperor of China to the Emperor of Japan in the ninth century.

There again, the cat was revered. Buddhists credited him with a soul.

It is often argued that the Abyssinian was the descendant of the Egyptian cat because the first subject, Zulma, was brought to England in 1868 after a military campaign in Abyssinia (now Ethiopia). This ticketed cat (ticking: each hair wears bands of different colors) was a huge success. Other subjects were found in many countries and used to create the race of the Abyssinians. Originally "Abyssinian" meant ticketed cat.

Scientific studies have examined the geographical distribution of ticketed cats. These studies have shown that the corresponding gene can't come from Africa, as the original home of these cats is located in south-east Asia. Research has shown that Zulma originally belonged to an officer of the Indian Army who had brought it with him to Abyssinia on his transfer to that country before handing it over to a comrade going back to England, Captain Barret-Lenhart.

The Siberian origin

The Turkish Angora appeared on the borders of Persia and Turkey, in the highlands (around Lake Van). Discovered by travelers, he was introduced into Europe in the seventeenth century. There was immediately a craze for this cat with its long silky fur. Very popular in aristocratic circles in the eighteenth century, it was considered a royal gift. Very quickly, he conquered the world and settled in many countries. He was used to create the different long-haired and semi-long-haired breeds, especially the Persian. In order not to interfere with the Persian breed, he was forbidden in shows. This resulted in his neglect and near-demise in Europe in the nineteenth century.

It is believed that the naturally semi-long-haired breeds (Angora Turkish, Norwegian, Siberian) have their origins in a distant adaptation of the first cat species to the harsh Siberian climate. They are believed to have spread to Norway and Turkey from their Siberian home.

It is thought he could be a descendant of the Manul cat, the wild species with the thickest fur. The comparison of the skulls of Manul cats and domestic cats disproves this, however.

The blue cats origin

Finally, the Chartreux cat, a blue cat with a thick though short-haired fur, is the descendant of cats brought during the Crusades as a result, it is said, of crossbreeding between the African cat and the Manul cat (a wild animal in which the blue color is common).

It was through the Chartreux cat that blue became a widespread colour in many breeds.

Conclusion about origins

Our domestic cats is a descendant of the Felis sylvestris wildcat, which is now falls into three subspecies: the European wildcat Felis sylvestris sylvestris, the African wild cat Felis sylvestris lybica, and the Asian wild cat Felis sylvestris ornata.

As can be seen, there is not only one geographical origin of our domestic cat. However, we can say that domestication began in Egypt, that from there it spread throughout Europe, that all European-type breeds find their origin there, and that, as a result of crossbreeding, all domestic breeds descend wholly or in part from Pharaonic cats.

First Maus Story

Princess Troubetzkoï's Maus

By the beginning of the twentieth century, Italy's feline population was made up of the descendants of the Egyptian cat. According to descriptions, a wide number of them were cats with spotted hair and resembling the pharaoh's cats.

Due to the Second World War, many cats died in Italy and the direct descendants of the pharaoh's cats practically disappeared. Nevertheless, spotted cats are still found in Italy and, it is said, also in Provence. In the movie "The Horseman on the Roof" (Jean-Paul Rappeneau), the feline hero has all the characteristics of the bronze mau.

On the contrary, the brown cat spotted in black seems to be still rather common in North Africa. Roadside cats looking like the bronze mau have been sighted even in Morocco. On the other side of Egypt, this kind of cat can be found also all along the Silk Road.

Nathalie Troubetzkoï was an exiled Russian princess who was led to live in Rome by the events in her life. Nathalie was really fond of cats. One day, a young boy brought her a kitten inside a cardboard box. The unusual beauty of this kitten did conquer her at once. The kitten was named Ludivine and nicknamed Ludol or Lulu. Lulu had a nice silvery fur adorned with black spots. The princess noted that the box which had contained the kitten was coming from Egypt. In this way she deduced the origin of this wonderful cat. She quickly understood that she had just met a descendant of the cats of the Pharaoh.

She alerted her numerous friends, asking them to find for her another cat of this type in order to get newborns with the same look. Some friends found her Gregorio, a black male, 11 years old, coming from a spotted family. Her friend, the ambassador of Syria, brought her an authentic specimen from the near East, called Geppa, a black smoke male.

Lulu and Geppa soon generated the first brood (1953) which was similarly spotted as their parents. Among them, Nathalie Troubetzkoï kept a small silver female, Baba. Later on, Gregorio made to Baba a few magnificent kittens, also spotted (1953), and, in between, a cat with a new color, Jojo, a bronze.

Nathalie Troubetzkoï began to make her cats known in Italy and went on in getting them reproduced. Liza (or Donna Lisa) was presented in a contest in Rome in 1955.

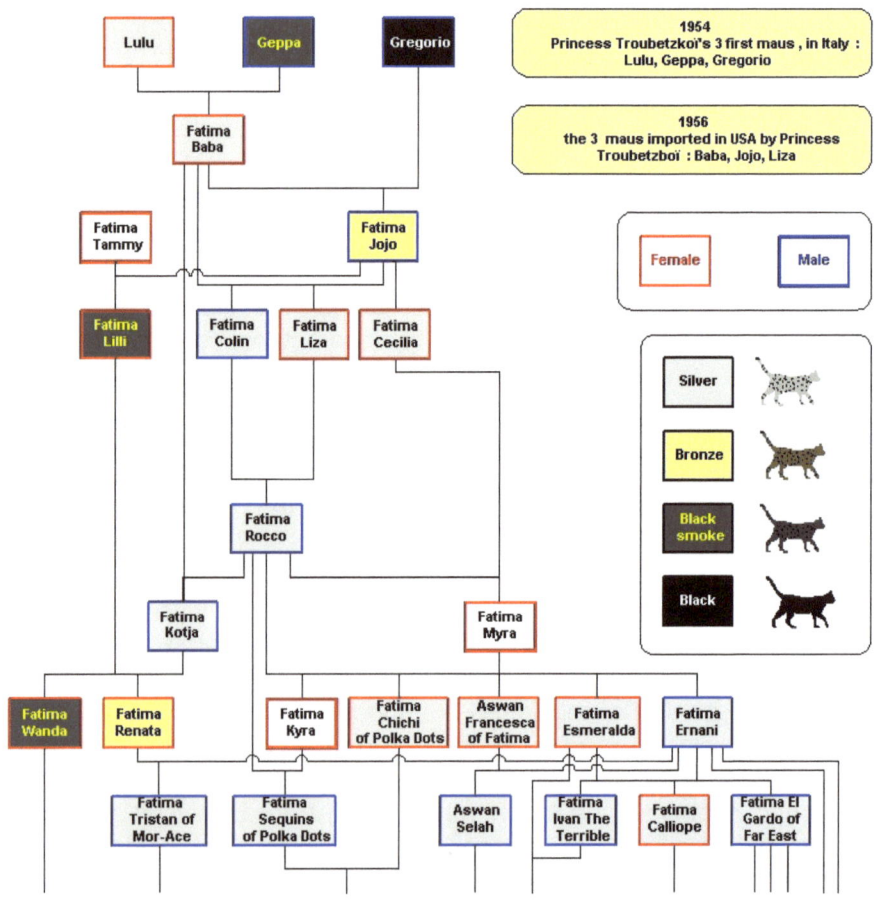

We have no information about Tammy: forgotten ancestors or new blood?

Let's mention Fatima André Chénier of Haj, Fatima Boris of Hydynasty, Fatima Ula of Trillium, Fatima Vito, Fatima Thais, Fatima Carlos, cats whose genealogy is now forgotten.

In 1956, she was, at last, authorized to emigrate to the USA. As she could not take all her cats with her, she had to choose three of them and found a home for the others. Thus it was that Baba, Jojo and Liza left for the conquest of the United States.

Once installed there, Nathalie Troubetzkoï went on promoting the Egyptian cats, exhibiting them and introducing them as a race under the name of the Egyptian Mau.

She created her own breeding under the name of Fatima, a cat house cat. In 1957, Baba was the first specimen of its race to be crowned champion. All bred Egyptian maus descend from the maus of the princess.

You can see above the genealogy of Princess Troubetzkoï's cats.

To breed a race starting from 3 original specimens is not an easy thing. Indeed, during several years, the breeders of the Egyptian mau were concerned about the Mau's consanguinity problems though external contributions were only few in numbers?

Oriental Spotted Tabby

Since the fifties, the British have been seduced by the Maus. Limited in their importation by quarantine rules, they tried to "recreate" the race starting from hybrids of Abyssinians, tabbies and Siamese cats. Initially, these cats were called Maus, but they have finally been recognized as a specific eastern variety: the Oriental spotted tabby.

That is why in some badly informed texts, we can sometimes read that the mau descends from the Siamese and that the morphologies of both cats are alike. Some errors are hard to die…

The first breeding

The Mau enjoying a tremendous success, other breeders bought some from the Princess and went in for breeding Maus. Their cats had great success in shows. However, the breed was not yet recognized, and Maus could not therefore claim any title. Among these early catteries are:

- Aswan   Frida St Sauveur & Helen Ware
- Bastis   Wain Harding & Bob Chorneau
- Far East   Jean Kryszczuk
- Haj   Jill Archibald
- Kattiwycke Ann Cahill
- Phiset   Mary Vail
- Polka Dots Susan Schwertley
- Sangpur   Shirley & Jean Charbonneau
- Trillium   Nathalie S. Smyth & Eric Prugh

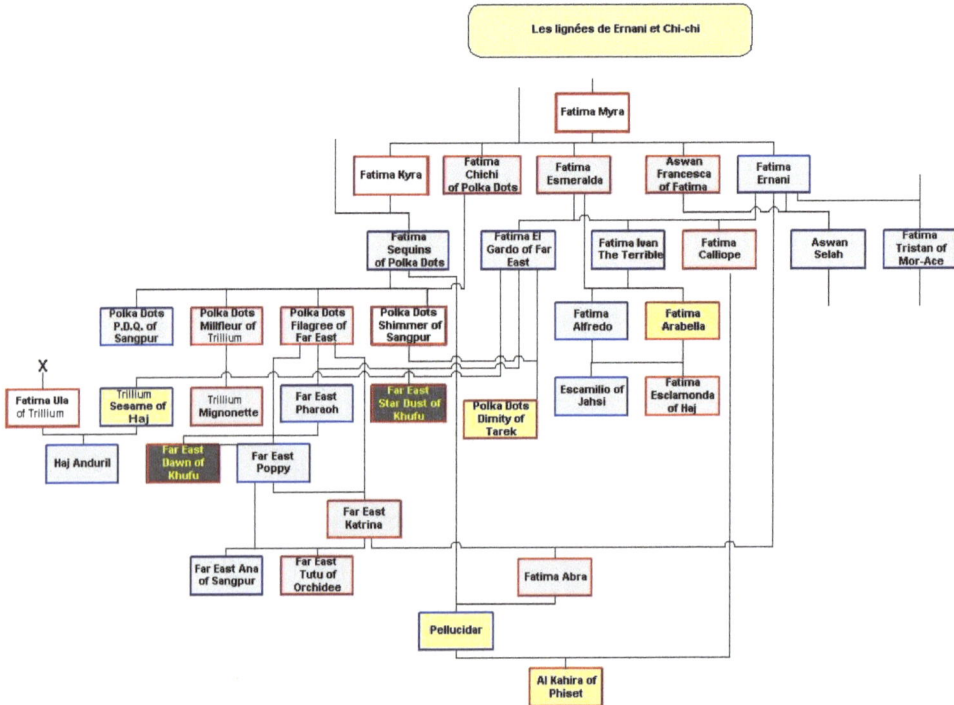

These early breeders as well as Princess Troubetzkoi did much to publicize the race. Thanks to them, Maus were accepted by the different U.S. feline organizations and were given a pedigree.

Finally, the Mau was recognized as a breed by the CFA (Cat Fanciers' Association) in 1977, by TICA (The International Cat Fanciers) in 1988 and FIFe (Fédération Internationale Féline) in 1992. Thanks to this recognition, he could finally obtain titles at cat shows.

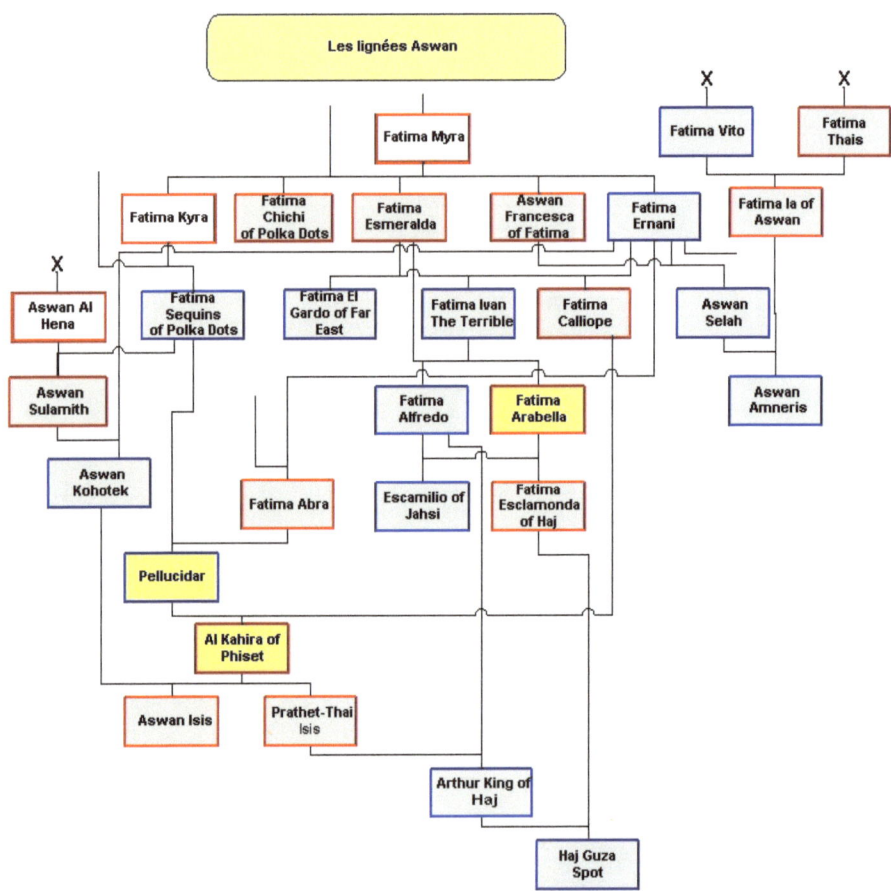

In 2004, GC's Tavaron Dotte Coolpepper played the role of the cat 'Midnight' in the film Catwoman.

The Indian line

In 1982, Jean Mill (Millwood cattery) made a trip to India. During this trip, the curator of the New Delhi zoo showed her a beautiful spotted bronze cat nestling between the legs of a sick rhinoceros. The cat had no tail: it had been accidentally crushed by a rhinoceros.

In itself, it was not surprising to find in India a distant descendant of the cats of the Pharaohs: historically, they accompanied caravans on the Silk Road.

Although this cat was pretty wild, Jean Mill brought it by plane to Los Angeles in a mahogany box marked "SAID TO BE A DOMESTIC CAT". Only a few days later the sex of the cat could be identified. It was a male, who was named Toby of New Delhi.

The curator of the New Delhi zoo also gave Jean Mill, Toby's sister, a female bronze, which was named Tasha of New Delhi.

At that time, Jean Mill was still breeding the Egyptian Mau and had initiated crossbreeding with Felis bengalensis to create the Bengal. Tobi and Tasha seemed perfect subjects for the fight against inbreeding in the Ocicat, the Egyptian Mau, the Bengals. Those familiar with the zoo in New Delhi must have noted that the rhinoceros enclosure is located in front of the Felis bengalensis cage...

Toby and Tasha could be registered with the American Cats Association. Considering the inbreeding problems that were becoming very worrying, the CFA agreed to recognize them as the Egyptian Mau. This decision was later postponed, then confirmed again.

Ocicats breeders were not interested in this new blood.

On the contrary Bengals breeders were very interested, and Toby and Tasha contributed greatly to the creation of the breed.

Many breeders of Egyptian Maus were reluctant, even hostile. In particular, Toby's wild character was considered worrisome for the future of the race. However, some breeders tried out the experiment. Thankfully, after a few generations, this wildness has softened, as expected. The offspring of Egyptian Mau Toby and Tasha is known as the Indian line.

Toby and Tasha have introduced a feature previously unknown in the Mau: the rufus polygene. It is this polygene that is responsible for the warm color of the Abyssinian. This polygene gives ~~to~~ the bronze Mau a very warm color, a little reddish. His critics describe him as 'tomato Mau', his line being more red-skin than Indian. Some purists prefer a traditional bronze, more yellow than red.

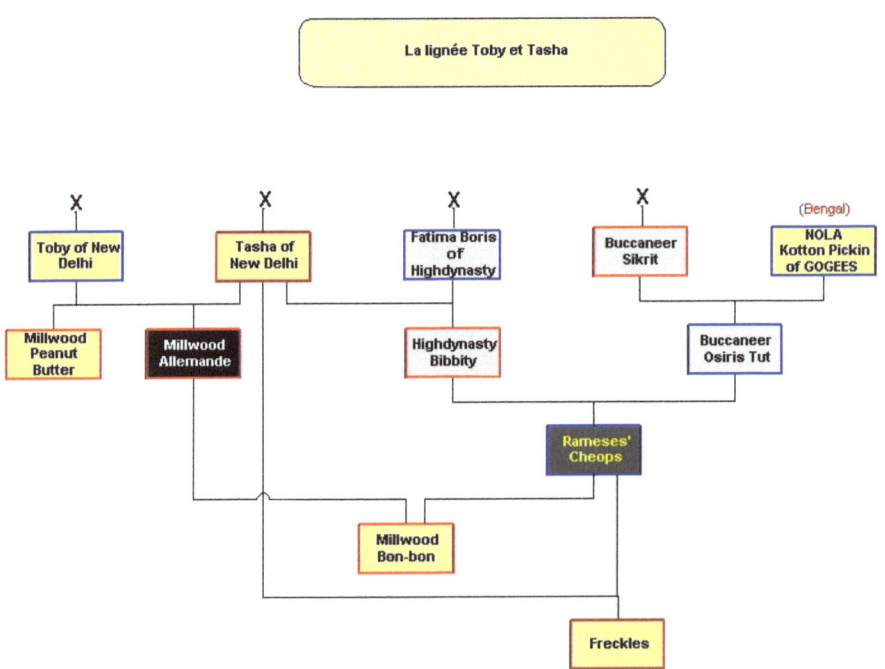

The first descendants of Toby and Tasha were often recorded both as Egyptian Mau and as Bengals (it was a non-official recording book because the race had not yet been recorded). Each ~~involved~~ cat involved was given two slightly different names as Mau and as Bengal (the difference often being a single letter), which helped to maintain some confusion. The pedigrees of Bengals highlight the use of it in some Maus lines at that time. Other breeds used to stabilize the Bengal breed (Burmese, American shorthair, domestic cat) are thus also found in these lines (but much less often).

Considering the Bengal cats born and also after examining pedigrees, there is good reason to believe that Toby was carrying the gene giving the marble pattern (see the chapter on genetics). Which is totally acceptable in the Bengal but is not accepted in the Mau: the

Mau must be spotted. In fact, traces of this gene can sometimes be found in the offspring of Toby.

The quality of Toby's contribution to the Egyptian Mau has been variable. The opinions of breeders on this issue differ.

The other Egypt imports

In the early 90s, other subjects from Egypt were introduced, especially by J. Len Davidson (Grandtrill) and Cathy Rowan (Rocat) and recognized by the CFA:

- *Hosny of Grandtrill*
- *Giza of Grandtrill*
- *Wasaya of Grandtrill*
- *Waafaya of Grandtrill*
- *Tarek of Jamila*

The line of Giza and Hosny have reached us.

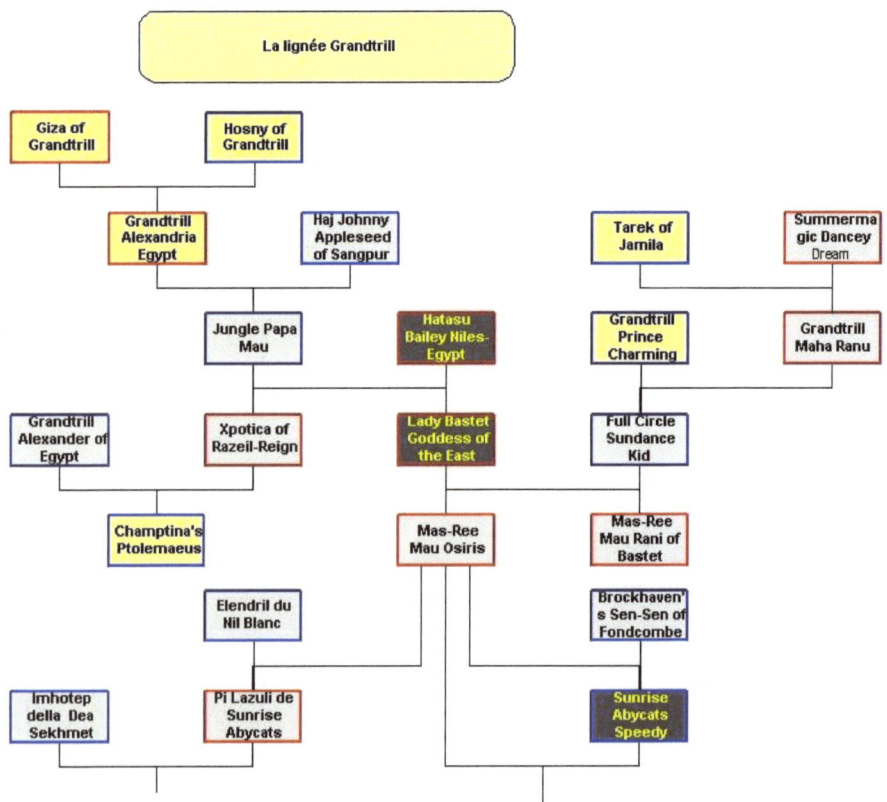

Sahourê

In 1999, Marie-Christine and Didier Hallépée travelled to Cairo to bring back a bronze Egyptian Mau, Sahourê. Sahourê was born into a human family and proved a sociable animal. Sahourê has been recognized in several international shows. His son, Senefer of Fondcombe, was supreme best at his first show...

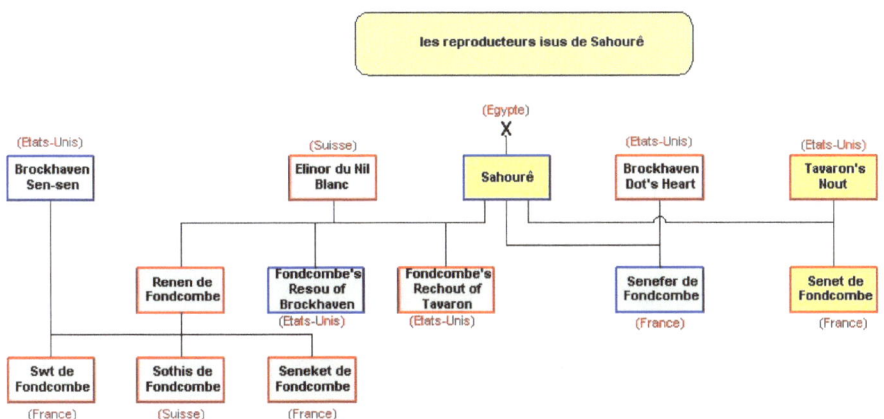

In 2000, a second trip to Cairo was organized in the hopes of bringing a female. Unfortunately, the cats that had been mentioned to them were not Maus. During their stay, at a market in Cairo, they were shown a little cat barely 2 months old and very angry. Once in Didier's arms, however, she calmed down and let herself ~~to~~ be looked at. The presence of red and white marks made her unfit to be recognized as Mau. They decided not to take her and left. Raafat, the taxi driver who was bringing them back to their hotel stopped on hearing a cat meowing. Having looked all over the taxi, they found the little cat clutching at the car axle: she had decided to follow them. So she had earned her plane ticket. Thus it was that Khalifa arrived in France, a Pharaonic cat, but not an Egyptian Mau.

Khalifa

In 2001, Didier Hallépée returned to Cairo. Again, the cats identified in advance proved unfit to be recognized. After much research, Didier managed to bring back a bronze female, Otta (cat in modern Egyptian) and a male bronze kitten, Maslama. Otta and Maslama were quite wild at first, but eventually settled down at home amid all the little band of Maus, and made no difficulty in accepting human presence, sometimes even settling on the bed. However, they remained reluctant to accept hand contact, but some little 'training' improved their behaviour.

Otta

A few weeks after her arrival, Otta exhibited a rounded belly. Thus were born of an unknown Egyptian father Totem (bronze male), Titus (bronze male) and Taboo (black male). Given their undesirable white spots, Otta and son were neutered. Taboo and Titus found a home: Though a little wild, they are soft and lovable. Totem shows the same qualities, but he soon realized that a visit meant the risk of having to leave soon one day so he remained hidden whenever visitors were in and didn't accept any contact, as if he had decided once and for all not to move house.

Maslama

As for Maslama, he was recognized by the CFA in 2003 and has also started his breeding career.

The Mau in Europe

After several attempts to introduce the Mau that did not succeed, there were finally 3 sustainable breedings:

- In Italy — de Joha cattery
  Rosella Perniola
- in Switzerland — von Dracusan cattery
  Hirsch
- In the Netherland — von Schooiertjes cattery
  Hans & Olga Garretsen

The presence of these three catteries created three areas where the Mau became known in Europe. Unfortunately, circumstances and geographic distance did not promote cooperation.

These Mau catteries have produced enough specimens to make the breed ~~to~~ emerge in Europe and to give other breeders the urge to embark on this adventure, especially in Europe.

In the 90s, Dianick Masson (Nil Blanc cattery) also began to interbreed Mau cats with cats from the von Dracusan and de Joha catteries.

In 1996, in Albi, Henry Cayssials, Vieux Pont cattery, purchased a couple from Rosiela Perniola. Henry Cayssials produced only one litter, then stopped breeding.

In 1997, the Hallépée family discovered the Mau in an article in Atout Chat Magazine. The breeder quoted in the article was Dianick Masson. So, Elendril du Nil Blanc and Élinor du Nil Blanc came to live at Fondcombe in the summer of 1997.

In 1998, Didier Hallépée created AIME, the International Association for the Egyptian Mau, to publicize the Mau in France and Europe and facilitate cooperation among breeders. Dianick Masson, Marie-Christine Hallépée and Stéphane Masson joined the venture. Within AIME, the number of breeders and cats produced has grown steadily since then and AIME has members in several European countries and in the United States.

In 1999, Melissa Bateson left the United States to return to ~~his~~ / her native England. She brought with her several of her Egyptian Maus from her Newkingdom Cattery. Due to enforcement of the quarantine, there was then no Mau in Britain. To be allowed to enter the country, her cats had to spend several months in a quarantine center, the one where the first English Egyptian Mau litter was born. Since then, Melissa has struggled a lot to publicize the race, get recognition by the Governing Council of Cat Fanciers (GCCF) and create new breeding centres. However, quarantine rules (which have not been removed in all countries) have long limited the introduction of new blood.

Some breeders in Holland and Germany are also grouped around Hans and Olga Garretsen (von Schooiertjes cattery) under the name of Maugang.

AIME

Presentation of AIME

AIME was founded in 1998 by Dianick Masson, Stephane Masson, Marie-Christine and Didier Hallépée Hallépée.

In 1997, the Mau was rare in Europe: a few breeders existed in Italy, in the Netherlands and in Switzerland. In Switzerland, at Dianick Masson's cattery (chatterie du Nil Blanc), Marie-Christine and Didier Hallépée (chatterie de Fondcombe) discovered this wonderful breed and decided to make it known in France. Under the impulse of Didier Hallépée, AIME was founded on February 20, 1998. They were soon joined by Sandrine Maisnier-Dufour (chatterie de Belenus) by Becki and Stephen Bergeron (Tavaron cattery) and by many others.

The purpose of AIME is the protection, promotion and breeding of the Egyptian Mau cat. As you can see, protection comes in first, breeding in last position. AIME certainly brings breeders together, but also Mau owners or even mere fanciers who have not yet decided to adopt a Mau. At AIME, the one important thing is not the owner or breeder of a Mau, it is the cat himself!

Our two main poles are naturally France and the United States. But AIME has (or had) members in Belgium, in the Netherlands, in Germany, in Switzerland, in Italy, in Denmark, in Finland and in Asia. AIME has also maintained relations with Britain, Luxembourg, Scandinavia, South America and Egypt. Thus, even if AIME has relations with LOOF, FIFe, CFA or TICA, it wants to preserve its independence and its values.

<u>Mau protection</u>
For AIME, the protection of the Mau means primarily the protection of its health and its quality of life. In the long term, it's a long fight against inbreeding: the Mau is 4,000 years old but is rare in breeding centers, which makes the fight against inbreeding difficult. But AIME succeeded in giving its Mau lines the health and the strength AIME was looking for.

Protection of the Mau ~~is~~ also means setting the best conditions for breeding and selling kittens in blooming health. It also chooses for the kittens homes where they can blossom surrounded by the love they deserve.

Finally, protection of the Mau means fighting against hybridization: AIME refuses any external input in the mau, who has lived through 4,000 years without ever needing it, and it refuses any use of the Mau to create or improve artificial breeds.

<u>Mau promotion</u>
Promoting the Mau is AIME's only means to make it known.

First, there is ~~first~~ the web site created by AIME in 1998: more than 1,000,000 pages seen in 7 languages. This is probably the most visited web site among those which are devoted to a breed of cats. On AIME breeders' web sites, more than 3 million pages have been seen since 1998.

Second, there is AIME's participation in various feline organizations: the Loof inFrance, FIFe, CFA and TICA. AIME participated directly or indirectly in the works of these organizations for standards definition and breed organization.

It is also participating in numerous shows. Obviously, AIME breeders are a mere handful and cannot go anywhere. But these breeders have exhibited in all regions of France and in many foreign countries: Italy, Switzerland, Portugal, Monaco, Luxembourg, Belgium, the Netherlands, Germany, Eastern Europe, the United States. Of course, some Maus acquired titles and have even won prestigious shows, but that's not the most important: what matters is to let you know the Mau and make you share our passion for this cat.

AIME was also involved in organizing special Egyptian Mau shows. We managed to collect up to 30 maus! To do this, breeders and owners have all had their share of the job. Just imagine so many beautiful cats available ~~to~~ for the public to look at them! All these colors side by side! It is also for members of AIME a great time of friendship around their common passion, the Mau. It is also an opportunity for me to see again these kittens that I had such trouble letting go away, and also their offspring, the fruit of (cat) generations of common work.

The better to share this passion, AIME has opened a forum, 'Maus d'amour' (Mau love). A whole program!

Mau breeding
For AIME, breeding is not an end in itself but a means to share our passion for the Egyptian Mau. We want happy cats. That's why we encourage family breeding and reject intensive breeding for our Maus.

We are very demanding with ourselves regarding the breeding conditions and sale of our kittens. We have assembled our best practices in a charter that our approved breeders conscientiously apply. No wonder the new owners remain with us in the association for a long time and continue to give us news for many years. Many of them have become my friends.

Obviously, you can breed cats another way and produce beautiful subjects. But our charter embodies values that we freely accept and share. For us, being a breeder approved by AIME is a label that has real value.

AIME Code of Ethic

The purpose of this document is to recall and clarify the key-points of our conception of breeding. Every applicant to the status of "A.I.M.E.-approved breeder", as well as any A.I.M.E. member registered as "Mau owner" and wishing to breed occasionally, must sign it, thus committing themselves to fulfill all its clauses.

Any dispute concerning its interpretation falls within the competence of the Board of Directors.

Skills
Allow for a minimum two-year experience in the breeding of the Egyptian Mau or another feline breed. Otherwise, accept a trial period of one year.

Sharing information
Communicate to AIME any information concerning:
➢ The registration of my cattery studbook number, Company Registration number, if applicable, Veterinarian Services registration number and, for France, the number of my Feline Capacity certificate.

- ➢ Number of owned cats (breed(s), breeding stock, sterilized cats) and possible changes.
- ➢ The identification of all my Egyptian Maus: pedigrees, tattoo or microchips numbers.
- ➢ The identification of my litters: pedigrees, tattoo or microchips numbers.
- ➢ The history of my cats before my membership, in particular the possible health problems encountered.

Legislation

Comply with the legislation of the country where I live and breed as regards breeding and shows.

Breeding conditions

- ➢ Offer my cat(s) a human and emotional presence that will ensure their welfare.
- ➢ Offer my cats large enough premises for a good quality of life and good sanitary conditions.
- ➢ Maintain no cat in a cage, except for health reasons or in case of absolute necessity.
- ➢ Never let my cat(s) wander. In case of uncontrolled wandering, it's recommended to have FelV and FiV tests performed on the return home of the cat and, if I have another cat, quarantine the absconder. In case these precautions were not applied, it is compulsory to have all the fugitive cats tested before putting them in contact with other cats (breeding, shows, boarding…).
- ➢ Try not to give a female oral or injectable contraception for more than three consecutive months.
- ➢ Avoid premature or repetitive pregnancies in order to protect the health of my breeding female cats.
- ➢ Give or sell no kitten under the age of three months.
- ➢ Allow any representative of the AIME Board to visit my breeding premises upon request.
- ➢ Never declaw any cat.

Acquisition of maus

- ➢ Inquire about the breeding conditions and, if possible, visit the cattery
- ➢ If possible, acquire only a fully inoculated cat having undergone the FelV and FiV tests. If not, have the tests and inoculations made as soon as possible and, in any case, before putting the animal in contact with other cats.
- ➢ Systematically have the cat examined by a veterinarian.

> If I have other cats, subject the newly arrived cat to an acclimatization period

Breeding

> Do no mating nor give stud services without the advice of AIME as regards the inbreed coefficients and the lines.
> When pregnancy is confirmed, inform AIME.
> In case of failed mating, inform AIME in order to extend the list of possible reproduction problems. For the same purpose, inform AIME of any problem that might occur during pregnancy.

Quality

> Allow every potential buyer to visit the totality of my breeding premises.
> Inform every potential buyer of the official standard and of the behavioral characteristics of the breed.
> Inform any potential buyer of any possible defect in a cat which is proposed to him for sale, and clearly explain the importance of this defect (e.g. in shows: penalties, disqualification).
> Guarantee every buyer a cat corresponding to the quality he asked for, that being of course subject to some possible characteristics that could appear later.
> Give to all buyers a hints note and stay at their disposal for any additional information or advice.

Prices and official documents

> Guarantee to every buyer a firm and definitive price, including, if need be, transport costs.
> Reduce the selling price in case a defect which was not visible at the time of the reservation should pop up.
> Consult A.I.ME. for any advice concerning the right price of a cat.
> France: never withhold pedigree or transfer of ownership until sterilization certificate is provided by the new owner. This is illegal.

Guarantees

Offer to every buyer of an Egyptian Mau cat from my cattery the following guarantees, without additional cost:

French breeders:

- ➢ Besides the legal guarantees provided for by the Code of Agriculture: FelV and FiV tests.
- ➢ Comply with the European legislation as regards documentation, rabies injections and delays when selling to foreign owners.

Breeder outside France:
- ➢ The legal guarantees provided for by the sanitary regulation of the country of origin of the kitten, as well as FelV and FiV tests.

Besides, tests of genetic filiation will be practised on all kittens and their results will be given to all buyers.

<u>Early sterilization (France)</u>
- ➢ Never spay a female aged less than 6 (six) months. Only early castration is allowed, as from the age of at least 3 months.
- ➢ Early castration will only be performed upon written request or with the written consent of the new owner. This sterilisation is made without additional cost if not performed at the buyer's specific request.

<u>Showing</u>
- ➢ Never show a female recently mated, even if pregnancy is not proved
- ➢ Never show a pre-reserved kitten without the future owner's explicit agreement.
- ➢ Never sell to unknown individuals during shows.
- ➢ Do not deliver a pre-reserved cat during a show if the buyer has never visited the cattery and is not already favourably known.

<u>Deontology</u>
- ➢ Forward to AIME head-office and/or to the other breeders any inquiries I could not satisfy.
- ➢ Forward to AIME any information concerning the Egyptian Mau breed, in order to improve my and AIME's knowledge.

AIME actions

Since its creation in 1998, AIME has been very active regarding the protection, promotion and breeding of the Egyptian Mau. Those who are familiar with the world of breeding or those who were interested in the Egyptian Mau were able to see that we worked hard and obtained considerable results. It has seemed to us interesting to summarize here our main actions.

The database
The Mau was introduced to breeding in 1954 by princess Troubetzkoï. To date, it adds up to several thousands of Maus and it is understandably quite difficult to retrace all the lineages. Marie-Christine HALLÉPÉE, our late president and founding member of the association, got down to this task and listed most of the breeding cats starting from the origins --- at least when the information could be found. This huge work gave birth to a database of about 4,000 Maus. It also allowed Didier HALLÉPÉE, vice-president and founding member of AIME, to establish the family trees of the first generations, those at the origin of the 'historic' lineages.

Besides its undeniable historic value, this database can also be seen as a precious genetic tool. It allows the computation of consanguinity rates between breeding cats over a number of significant generations (around ten) in order to minimize unwanted impacts. It also allows tracking undesirable genes in order to avoid the appearance of undesirable characteristics such as the blotched or the rufus (see below) and to preserve the Mau's unique beauty. Finally - precautionary principle - it can help in detecting and eliminating some regrettably too classic genetic diseases that usually appear when the practices of breeding are not optimal but which fortunately have not yet struck the Mau.

The fight against consanguinity
Breeding of the Mau started with 3 subjects imported by princess Troubetzkoï: Gregorio, Geppa and Lulu. With such a start, consanguinity was an unavoidable phenomenon. However, numerous generations later, a sensible choice of breeding cats allows us now to obtain acceptable rates (less than 10 %).

Consanguinity can be a tool of selection to highlight such and such characteristics. It's very much appreciated (and used) by breeders who privilege beauty and want to perform well at shows. Why not? But consanguinity also tends to highlight unwanted characteristics and, if used in excess, it weakens the lineages. As regards the Mau, endemic consanguinity became quite upsetting in the past. That's why AIME has always strongly fought against consanguinity and established strict principles which were followed by our breeders, the result being that after years of constant drop in consanguinity rates, they are now stabilized at a very low level. Thanks to that policy, our cats are sturdy, of dazzling health and stable character. We noticed that when reverse principles were applied, the lineages could present the very problems which we wanted to avoid.

The introduction of fresh blood
In order to fight against consanguinity, we introduced new subjects from Egypt. Indeed, is there a better or more natural way than to go back to the source and get authentic descendants of the cats of the Pharaohs?

Of course, it's not that easy. Over 4,000 years, the Egyptian feline population has greatly diversified and in a country where the breeding of cats doesn't exist, to say the least, it's hard to find subjects both presenting all the characteristics of the Mau and devoid of undesirable characteristics that could spread genetically.

Marie-Christine and Didier HALLÉPÉE got down to this task. In 1999, they brought back from Egypt a magnificent male, Sâhouré de Fondcombe, which was shown in exhibits in France and in Germany where it was recognized as an authentic Bronze Egyptian Mau by renowned international judges.

In 2003, Didier HALLÉPÉE went back to Egypt in order to get Otta de Fondcombe and Maslama de Fondcombe. Otta was neutered after her one single litter ever. As for Maslama, he followed Sâhouré's good example.

These Egyptian cats are magnificent bronze-colored cats of an exceptional stature. As for character, one can find all the characteristics of the Bronze Egyptian Mau, possibly even accentuated.

Their use in the association's breeding programs allowed us to achieve our goal: bring down the consanguinity rate as close to zero as possible. Their non-intensive use in our breeding programs also helped us not to recreate the conditions of a new wave of consanguinity.

Coming directly from Egypt, they showed (as expected) a stronger and more feline character. But according to our expectations, their offspring significantly softened while still preserving the strong personality of the Bronze Mau. The beauty and character of their children and grandchildren allowed some of them to participate in shows and win titles (proof of their beauty and obedience). One of them, Senefer, even succeeded in becoming a Best Supreme in one of those shows.

Quite a few Maus in the United States originate from Sâhouré's and Maslama's offspring.

The work on standards
Thanks to the relations AIME keeps with the whole world of the Egyptian Mau, we have acquired a rare knowledge of the standards currently observed in the various feline associations: Loof, CFA, Tica, FIFe. So, when Loof decided to update its standards, we participated in its work and helped to take into account the small differences which could exist between them. Our work also emphasized what differentiates the Mau from the other races and what undesirable characteristics could be introduced by hybridization. The new Loof standard takes into account the work of the association.

The promotion and protection of the Bronze Mau
The Bronze Mau was, for a long time, the least appreciated Mau in France. Fewer in numbers, it was rarely shown in shows. Less spectacular than the Silver Mau, it was also less popular.

From the start, AIME's work was aimed at giving the Bronze Mau too ~~could find~~ its letters of nobility. It was shown in shows as often as possible and was systematically present during Breed Specials where it rose to the first places.

The beauty of its patterns perfectly distinguishes it from the house cat. Its coat is bronze-colored with yellow sub-hair and black spotted patterns. The most beautiful are effectively contrasted on a warm color, just like the cats of the Pharaohs which we have often met in Egypt. A colder shade of bronze, however, remains magnificent.

In the 80's, an American breeder used the Egyptian Mau to create the Bengal. Subtle choices of breeding led on the one hand to the

Bengals and on the other hand to the 'Indian' lineage, represented by Bronze Egyptian Maus strongly tinged with red (rufus). For a long time, these two types were sometimes difficult to differentiate from each other until the Bengal stabilized in accordance with its current standard.

In the United States, the main associations recognized either the Mau or the Bengal. The risks of confusion thus mattered little.

Bronze Mau and Bengal are nowadays two fully differentiated breeds and this difference is well in evidence in the standard of the Bronze Mau. This distinction allows protecting the existence of two magnificent cats which have each their specific beauty.

As for the public, it fully appreciates the authentic aspect of the Bronze Mau, which so very strongly reminds us of the feline representations which can be found on antique Egyptian monuments, as well as its very pronounced feline character.

The recognition of the Black Mau
The color of the Mau is determined by 2 genes. It thus produces 4 colors: Silver, Bronze, Black Smoke, Black.

Silver is the most spectacular color. The public is extremely sensitive to it!

Bronze is the most authentic color: 4,000 years of Egyptian tradition and a very strong feline character.

Black Smoke (smoke grey with silvery sub-hair and black-spotted patterns) is the subtlest color of the four, revealed by lighting effects. Its character is softer, but it tends to be aloof with strangers.

And, for a long time, the standards were limited to these 3 colors. The unfortunate Black Mau, the victim of the rigours of the genetics, used to be thought unworthy of the name of Mau and its reproduction even used to be forbidden. Obviously, black on black is not spectacular. Its sweetness, even more pronounced than that of the Black Smoke, did not bring to light its feline authenticity! Let's note that in the United States, CFA recognizes the Black Mau in the breeding programs but not in the shows.

AIME obtained the recognition of the Black Mau. This wonderful companion is henceforth fully recognized, authorized for reproduction and can even participate in shows under NRC (New Breeds and Colors). But it can't aspire to any titles.

Given its rarity, it will be difficult for you to get one, but you must know that it's a magnificent companion worthy of being put on a par with its more contrasted friends.

The conservation of the standard
A completely pure race doesn't exist: there are always some recessive genes which the selection can rarefy but never totally eliminate. The corresponding characteristics can then re-appear. Sometimes, the clumsiness or inexperience of a breeder can facilitate this resurgence.

With the Mau, we sometimes have kittens which, far from being spotted, present a marbled pattern called blotched. The first characteristic of the Mau being to be spotted (even in black on black), this pattern is banned. The kitten thus cannot be considered as a Mau. It is, however, a magnificent companion which will make the enjoyment of its new family.

It came to our attention that some people declared this type of cat as Mau and made them reproduce even if it meant perpetuating the presence of this pattern in the race. Others in France wish to see this pattern recognized. For AIME, such recognition is not desirable and it's a practice against which we fight.

Red color (rufus polygene) in the Bronze Mau also goes against the standard. It's passed on from generation to generation, is difficult to eliminate, and gives the Silver Mau unwanted reddish colorings.

For these reasons, AIME fights for the respect of the standard which represents the characteristics of the race. Some people might feel free to try out all the 'improvements' about which they dream, but let them not have any trial with the Mau nor should they use it. 4,000 years of tradition deserve an effort of continuity.

DNA Tests
Our magnificent cats are kind, obedient, and so on. They would never dream of reproducing in secret, without letting their breeders know it, even with a cat of another race. Only in a Walt Disney cartoon can we see Duchess choose Tom O' Malley, the alleycat!

Of course, accidents can happen. As the genetic characteristics of the Mau are almost always dominant, the breeder can even be deceived by the appearance of kittens.

The seriousness of our breeders makes this type of involuntary error improbable. But the potential buyer is entitled to a guarantee rather than to nice words.

Henceforth, genetic tests make it possible to prove in an unquestionable way the filiation of cats at a reasonable cost.

This is why AIME asks its approved breeders to offer their buyers the guarantee of filiation offered by the genetic tests.

The sharing of experience
AIME is a human-sized association. So all information is shared and that sharing is made even easier by the fact that friendly relations unite us.

So, we have set our hearts on sharing our feline experiences. This sharing enriches our knowledge and helps us all implement the best policies and easily resolve small or big problems which may appear, for the biggest profit of our companions.

Shows and specials
AIME encourages its breeders and cat owners to participate in numerous shows in France and abroad to make our magnificent companion better known.

Furthermore, we sometimes participate in the organization of Egyptian Mau specials, great moments that allows us to meet amongst friends together with our 4-legged companions for the biggest pleasure of the public.

Although there is only a handful of us, we were on a few occasions able to gather up to 30 Maus of all colors and origins.

These various specials are also a strong moment in the lives of our feline judges. Furthermore, they allow us to measure the progress of our breeders in view of the increasing quality of the shown subjects.

The Newsletter
Since 1998, AIME has been publishing a small newspaper in the French and English languages for the benefit of its members.

This newsletter allows us to strengthen the link which unites us together and contributes to the memory of the association.

Some figures

Mau births in France: around 30 a year
Mau births in the world: around 300 a year

Maus in France: around 300
Maus in the world: around 5000

THE COLORS OF THE MAU

The classical ones:
silver, bronze, black smoke and black

Since his origin, the Mau exists in four colors:

- *silver*
- *bronze*
- *black smoke*
- *black*

silver

The coat is gray with a white undercoat, the spotted marks are black.
This is the most known and most spectacular color.

bronze

The coat is yellow, the spotted marks are black.
This is the traditional color of the cat of pharaohs.
According to some standards, the color can range from yellow to red with black spots.

black smoke

The coat is smoked gray, the spotted marks are black.
This is told the most the subtle color.

black

The coat is solid black.
The black Mau is not admitted at show. He is accepted for breeding in CFA. He has been recognized in France in 2006.

Since the first Maus, the 4 colors have been present.

The 3 first Maus of Princess Troubetzkoï were:
- Lulu   *silver female*
- Geppa   *black smoke male*
- Gregorio   *noir male*

The 3 Maus imported in the United-States by Princess Troubetzkoï were:
- Baba   *silver female*
- Jojo   *bronze male*
- Liza   *silver female*

In the case of the black smoke, only the base of the hair is colored. In the absence of selection, the colored area is more or less large (depending on the rate of melanin). If the rate of melanin is very low, the cat looks solid with a silver undercoat (which appears when you fluff the hair). Otherwise, ghost black spots are visible on a smoky gray coat with silver undercoat.

By means of selection the marking can be fixed in a given breed. In breeds other than the Egyptian Mau, the standards require a solid coat without ghost marking for smoke cats. By contrast, for the Egyptian Mau, the preference is for a coat with ghost spots.

Scientific studies have shown that, in the cat, colors not encountered in the wild are related to a more sociable character. This explains why breeders have found that black smoke Maus (and, even more so, black Maus) have the softest temper of all.

The blue

The presence of a recessive gene for dilution may change the base color of the Mau from black to blue. /

The Mau can comes in four new colors based on blue: blue-silver, blue spotted, blue smoke, blue self.

CFA recognizes these cats since 1977 (AOV status: recognized but not allowed in show).

The blue Maus are not recognized in France.

The number of known blue Maus is extremely low.

The Shirazi

In Egypt exist some long-hair Maus. They are known under name of Shirazi.

By this time, no standard recognize them yet.

Genetic elements

Generalities on genetic

The characteristics specific to living species and differences specific to individuals in each species are listed in the genes that make up the chromosomes.

Each species has a fixed number of chromosomes (19 pairs for cats, 23 pairs for humans). Half the genetic material comes from the father, the other half from the mother.

Each gene is present on each of two chromosomes. A gene will be called dominant when its presence in one of two chromosomes is sufficient to express the character it bears. A gene is called recessive when its presence on both chromosomes is necessary to express the character it bears. Dominant genes are represented by capital letters, recessive genes by lower-case letters. When both alleles of the gene (the components on each of two chromosomes) are identical, it is called homozygotous. When they are different, it is called heterozygotous.

The sex chromosome transmits sex. The female chromosome is symbolized by X, the male chromosome by Y. A female carries two X chromosomes (she's XX) and can transmit only X chromosomes to her offspring. A male carries one X chromosome and one Y chromosome (he's XY) and can pass on either an X chromosome or a Y chromosome

The sex chromosome has a characteristic: the X chromosome has more genes than the Y chromosome. Concerning genes on sex chromosomes, the female therefore has 2 genes while the male has only one. So some traits can be specific to one sex.

Transmission of genes

When we cross two subjects, one would like to know how to transmit a given character by observing the transmission of genes.

Let's take a gene called G, for example; each parent carries a component of the gene on each of his or her two chromosomes. The dominant form of the gene is symbolized by G and the recessive form by g; each individual will be GG, Gg, gG, or gg. Gg and gG are equivalent (no matter who originates a specific gene).

During reproduction, each parent will transmit only one gene. For example, if the father has the form G1 and G2 of the G gene and the mother forms G3 and G4 of the G gene, we have:

	G1	G2
G3	G1 G3	G2 G3
G4	G1 G4	G2 G4

This means that children may be present (with equal probability) the combinations above.

Examples

Crossing two individuals homozygous for a given gene
(GG crossed with GG)

	G	G
G	GG	GG
G	GG	GG

Result: all individuals are homozygous in the same gene, like their parents

Crossing an individual homozygous for the dominant gene with a heterozygous individual
(GG crossed with Gg)

	G	G
G	GG	GG
g	Gg	Gg

Result: all individuals carry the dominant gene (they resemble their parents for this trait). Half of them are homozygous.

Crossing an individual homozygous for the recessive gene with a heterozygous individual
(gg crossed with Gg)

	g	g
G	Gg	Gg
g	gg	gg

Result: half the people carry the dominant gene (they show the dominant trait) but are heterozygotous (they can transmit the recessive trait). The other half expresses the recessive trait.

Crossing two heterozygous individuals
(Gg crossed with Gg)

	G	g
G	GG	Gg
g	Gg	gg

Result: one child in four will express the recessive gene that was present but hidden from each parent. Among others, one in 3 of them will be homozygous for that gene.

Rules to remember

For a given gene:
- If an individual expresses the dominant character, he or she carries a least one corresponding gene
- If an individual expresses the recessive trait, he or she carries two recessive genes
- If at least one child expresses the recessive trait, both parents carry this recessive gene
- If a child is gg, each parent carries g
- If a parent expresses the recessive trait, each child will at least carry this recessive gene
- If one parent is gg, each child carries g

Statistical rules

For a given gene:
- The crossing of an individual carrying the recessive trait with an individual homozygous for this recessive trait gives 50% of children in each of the two traits
- Gg + gg → 50% Gg and 50% gg
- The crossing of two individuals carrying the recessive trait gives 25% of children expressing the recessive trait. Among those expressing the dominant trait, 1/3 is pure.
- Gg + Gg → 75% G? and 25% gg
- Among children G?, 1/3 is GG and 2/3 is Gg

Cat genetics

The known part of the genetics of the cat focuses on the coat (texture and color.)

L gene: hair length
Dominant form: short hair
Recessive form: long hair

Hr gene: presence of hair
Dominant form Hr: normal hair
Recessive form hr: lack of hair (Sphinx)

R gene: Cornish Rex texture
Dominant form A: normal hair
Recessive form r: Cornish Rex texture (short and wavy hair and no guard hair)

Gen Re: Devon Rex texture
Dominant form Re: normal hair
Recessive form re: Devon Rex texture (short and wavy hair)

Gene Wh: wire hair
Dominant form Wh: wire hair (very curly, hard to the touch)
Recessive form wh: normal hair

W gene: dominant white (White)
This gene affects the rate of production of melanin. In the W form of the gene, the rate of melanin is low, so the cat is white.

Dominant form W: the cat is white
Recessive form w: the cat's coat is colored.

If the rate of melanin is very low, eye color is blue. If the rate of melanin is too low, the internal ear is affected and the cat is deaf.

Melanin may be unevenly distributed. The cat may then have odd eyes (one blue eye and one colored eye). The ear on the side of the blue eye can be deaf.

When the cat is heterozygous Ww (we then say 'color bearer'), the rate of melanin is enough for the cat is not deaf. In this case, the kitten at birth have a spot of color on the forehead, a spot that disappears after a few days.

B gene: Base Color
This gene controls the base color of the cat's coat

Dominant form B:	the base color is black or dark brown
Recessive form b:	the background color is chocolate
Recessive form b1:	the background color is cinnamon

C gene: color distribution
This gene controls the distribution of melanin pigment throughout the body

Dominant form C:	the whole body is colored
Recessive form c:	albino with red eyes (usually non-viable)
Recessive form ca:	albino blue eyes
Recessive form cb:	color attenuated on the body but not on the extremities
Recessive form cs:	only the extremities are colored (Siamese pattern)

Ch gene: Chinchilla

Dominant form Ch:	Chinchilla (the pattern is not visible or ghost)
Recessive form ch:	non Chinchilla (the pattern is visible)

Gene A: Agouti
This gene controls the distribution of melanin in the hair, and so the expression of the pattern on the coat.

Dominant form A:	agouti (the pattern is visible)
Recessive form a:	not agouti (the pattern is not visible or ghost)

The ghost pattern result from the distribution of melanin at the base of the hair. This distribution is due to polygenes.

I gene: inhibition
This gene controls the presence of the pigment at the base of the hair.

Dominant form I: inhibited: silver undercoat
Recessive form i: uninhibited: colored undercoat

In the Black Cat, the undercoat is yellow. In the presence of this gene, the undercoat is white (silver). The color of the cat is then silver (agouti cat) or smoke (non-agouti cat).

D gene: dilution
This gene controls the color intensity

Dominant form D: natural color
Recessive form of: diluted color

In the presence of this gene, black becomes blue, brown becomes lilac, fawn becomes light brown, and red becomes cream.

Ta gene: ticking)
This gene controls the distribution of bands of color on the hair of agouti cats.

Dominant form Ta: Ticking or abyssinian: All hair is agouti. Only one band appears on the back, and each hair wears stripes of different colors giving the cat's coat the characteristic appearance of the hare, as in the Abyssinian.
Recessive form ta: the number of color bands of each hair is limited and appearance is not characteristic of the hare.

In the presence of the dominant form of this gene, the pattern of the coat is hidden by the ticking. In its absence, the pattern of the coat can be expressed.

Mc gene: Coat pattern (striped or mackerel)
This gene controls the distribution of agouti hairs, and therefore the pattern of the coat.

Dominant form Mc: tabby or mackerel: robe covered with stripes as in wild felines.
Recessive form mc: blotched (also called classic tabby): The coat has large patterns that are not stripes.

In spotted cats, the spots in principle follow the design of the original stripes. Stripes may remain (vertical stripes on the sides). If the cat has the mc gene (blotched), horizontal stripes may also occur.

Sp Gene: coat pattern (Spotted)

The presence of this gene breaks the pattern of the coat, which is expressed as spots.

Dominant form Sp:	Spotted: the pattern is interrupted giving the cat a spotted pattern. The spots in principle follow the design of the original stripes. Stripes may remain on the flanks.
Recessive form sp:	the pattern is not interrupted. The original motive is expressed.

So:

Mc - Sp -	spotted tabby background spots are aligned vertically
Mc - spsp	or mackerel tabby
mcmc Sp -	spotted background spots are aligned rather horizontally
mcmc spsp	marbled or blotched (Also called "classic tabby)

If both parents carry the recessive allele sp, non-spotted kittens may appear. These kittens can be mackerel or blotched.

S gene: White spots (white spotting)

This gene controls the presence of more or less extensive white spots.

Dominant form S:	presence of white spots
Recessive form s:	no white spots

The extent and distribution of spots depends on polygenes, which are still poorly understood. In black cats, this gene is frequently expressed by a neck mark (the mark of the angel or the finger of God) and a string.

O gene: Red

This gene is carried by the sex chromosome X. It therefore expresses itself differently in males and females.

Form 1 O: base color tinted orange (red)
Form 2 O':   base color undyed orange (eg black)

This gives for the male (XY):

Genotype O   red cat
Genotype O'   non-red cat (eg black)

And for the female (XX):

Genotype OO: red cat
Genotype O'O': non-red cat (e.g. black)
Genotype OO':   cat with red areas and non-red areas (tortie, blue cream, etc.).

If a male is tortoiseshell (red and black), its genotype is XXY instead of XY. This genetic defect (uncommon but not rare) makes the cat impotent.

In the 90s, in the United States, a house cat had a great success in CFA shows: he was black, red, blue and cream. Her dress expressed both dilution and non-dilution: a genetic defect probably due to a supernumerary dilution gene.

The genetics of Mau

The presence of recessive genes in a breed is unavoidable, even when not wished. These genes can come from the original gene pool of the breed as well as from input intended to improve such or such a character, or from breeding accidents.

When a character is not wished in the breed standard, it is gradually eliminated by the selection made by breeders.

In some cases, the presence of this recessive gene is too widespread for the gene to be completely eliminated.

As regards genes whose presence in the recessive form has not been proved in the breed, we will consider the Mau as relatively pure and for convenience sake we will note the presence of two dominant genes. When the value of the gene is unknown, we shall note it as x.

Sp Gene: coat pattern (Spotted)

The presence of this gene breaks the pattern of the coat, which is expressed through spots.

Dominant form Sp:	Spotted: the pattern is interrupted giving the cat a spotted pattern. The spots in principle follow the design of the original stripes. Stripes may remain on the flanks.
Recessive form sp:	the pattern is not interrupted. The original motive is expressed.

L gene	hair length	LL	Short hair
Hr gene	presence of hair	HrHr	Normal hair (not nude cat)
R gene	Cornish Rex texture	RR	Normal hair (not Cornish Rex)
Re gene	Devon Rex texture	ReRe	Normal hair (not Devon Rex)
Wh gene	wire hair	WhWh	Normal hair (not wired)
W gene	dominant white	ww	Not white
B gene	base color	BB	Black or dark brown
C gene	color distribution	CC	Color all over the body (no Siamese pattern)
Ch gene	Chinchilla	chch	Not Chinchilla
A gene	Agouti		A: silver or bronze a: black smoke or black
I gene	Inhibition		I: silver or black smoke i: bronze or black
D gene	Dilution		Usually DD for the Mau. The blue color is recognized by CFA but not admitted in show.
Ta gene	Ticking	tata	The Mau is not ticketed as Abyssinian. The tabby marking can be seen.
Mc gene	Coat pattern	mcmc	The spotted pattern is expressed in the Mau. It is not hidden by a tabby pattern.
Sp gene	Coat pattern (Spotted)	Sp -	The Mau is always spotted. This is the characteristic of the breed. The recessive

			gene can still be found within the breed. When the recessive gene sp appears, the mc gene can express and the kitten is blotched instead of spotted. It is no more a Mau.
S gene	White spotting	ss	Le mau devrait ss. Cependant, les taches blanches existent dans la race et ressortent dans les lignées sous l'action de polygènes. Le gène S est difficile à éliminer. La présence de taches blanches sur le corps est un défaut chez le mau.
O gene	Red	O'Y ou O'O'	Neither red nor tortoise. The reddish color of some Maus doesn't come from this gene but from rufus polygenes

So, the only three genes that may change in the Mau are A, I, D.

When you give the genotype of a Mau, you only specify the A and I genes. You specify the D gene only for blue Maus.

- Ax Ix   *silver   visible pattern,*
  silver undercoat
- Ax ii   *bronze visible pattern,*
  classic undercoat (yellow)
- aa Ix   *black smoke   ghost pattern,*
  silver undercoat
- aa ii   *black   solid black color*

- Ax Ix dd   *silver blue   visible blue pattern,*
  silver undercoat
- Ax ii dd   *bronze blue   visible blue pattern,*
  classic undercoat (yellow)
- aa Ix dd   *smoke blue   ghost blue pattern*
  silver undercoat
- aa ii dd   *solid blue   solid blue color*

Blue Maus are not recognized in France.

Colors crossing

To anticipate the colors produced when crossing two Maus, it's necessary to know their genotypes:

- ➤ AA II   pure silver
- ➤ Aa II   silver wearing smoke
  (can produce smoke)
- ➤ AA Ii   silver wearing bronze
  (can produce bronze)
- ➤ Aa Ii   silver wearing bronze and smoke
- ➤ AA ii   pure bronze
- ➤ Aa ii   bronze wearing smoke
- ➤ aa II   pure black smoke
- ➤ aa Ii   black smoke wearing bronze
- ➤ aa ii   black

		SILVER				BRONZE		SMOKE		BLACK
		AA II	Aa II	AA Ii	Aa Ii	AA ii	Aa ii	aa II	aa Ii	aa ii
S I L V E R	AA II	silver	silver	silver	silver	silver	silver	silver	silver	silver
	Aa II	silver	¾ silver ¼ smoke	silver	¾ silver ¼ smoke	silver	¾ silver ¼ smoke	½ silver ½ smoke	½ silver ½ smoke	½ silver ½ smoke
	AA Ii	silver	silver	¾ silver ¼ bronze	¾ silver ¼ bronze	½ silver ½ bronze	½ silver ½ bronze	silver	¾ silver ¼ bronze	½ silver ½ bronze
	Aa Ii	silver	¾ silver ¼ smoke	¾ silver ¼ bronze	9/16 silver 3/16 smoke 3/16 bronze 1/16 black	½ silver ½ bronze	3/8 silver 3/8 bronze 1/8 smoke 1/8 black	½ silver ½ smoke	3/8 silver 3/8 smoke 1/8 bronze 1/8 black	¼ silver ¼ bronze ¼ smoke ¼ black
B R O N Z E	AA ii	silver	silver	½ silver ½ bronze	½ silver ½ bronze	bronze	bronze	silver	½ silver ½ bronze	bronze
	Aa ii	silver	¾ silver ¼ smoke	½ silver ½ bronze	3/8 silver 3/8 bronze 1/8 smoke 1/8 black	bronze	¾ bronze ¼ black	½ silver ½ smoke	¼ silver ¼ bronze ¼ smoke ¼ black	½ bronze ½ black
S M O K E	aa II	silver	½ silver ½ smoke	silver	½ silver ½ smoke	silver	½ silver ½ smoke	smoke	smoke	smoke
	aa Ii	silver	½ silver ½ smoke	¾ silver ¼ bronze	3/8 silver 3/8 smoke 1/8 bronze 1/8 black	½ silver ½ bronze	¼ silver ¼ bronze ¼ smoke ¼ black	smoke	¾ smoke ¼ black	½ smoke ½ black
B L A C K	aa ii	silver	½ silver ½ smoke	½ silver ½ bronze	¼ silver ¼ bronze ¼ smoke ¼ black	bronze	½ bronze ½ black	smoke	½ smoke ½ black	black

Obviously, in many cases the genotype of the parents is not known. So, it is necessary to wait for the birth of the kittens and then observe those which have just been born.

STANDARDS

At shows cats are judged in accordance to a standard corresponding to their breed.

The different cat associations have their own standard. The best known are the Cat Fanciers' Association (CFA), The International Cat Association (TICA), the Fédération Internationale Féline (FIFe). The standards of these three associations have been references in the feline world for a long time. They are available on the Internet.

In France, the law of January 6, 1999 provided for the creation of a single stud book for the French feline world. The creation of this book has led to the adoption of a common standard. The project is managed by LOOF. LOOF consulted the various breed clubs and the specialized judges to improve their standards. It is the version 01/01/2007 LOOF standards developed with the participation of AIME that we present below.

Permissible colors

Black silver spotted tabby, brown spotted tabby (bronze), black smoke, black.

Category: traditional Divisions: solid, tabby (spotted tabby pattern only), and silver/smoke (smoke and spotted tabby pattern only)

Colors: black

Since January 2006, the black Mau is allowed in new color (NC).

NC: new colors can be shown in cat shows but are not eligible to certificates nor take part in Best in Shows. They are judged and can obtain an excellent if the subject presented is of sufficient merit.

Introduction

The Egyptian Mau is a natural spotted domestic breed. This medium sized cat combining power and elegance strikes by the contrast between its short and lustrous coat and the expression of its shiny green eyes.

Head

Medium, the head is a modified wedge with soft contours without any flat plane. From the front, the cheeks are not full, except in males who often have jowls. The nose is even in width throughout length. From the side, the forehead is slightly rounded and followed by a gentle concave curve at eye level. The nose is straight.

Muzzle

Neither short nor long, the softly rounded muzzle blends with overall head shape. The chin is firm, neither protruding nor receding.

Eyes

Almond-shaped, the eyes are large and well-open and set at a bias without being oriental. The ideal color is gooseberry green.

Ears

Medium to large, the ears are wide at base, rounded at tip and set rather apart following the lines of the head. Viewed in profile, they are set rather at the back of the head. The ears are covered with very short hair at the back and the inside is almost transparent. Lynx tips are accepted.

Neck

Well-defined, the neck is arched.

Body

Semi-foreign in type, the body is medium, with well-balanced combination of power and elegance. Shoulders are prominent and angulated. Musculature is well developed, especially in adult males which may be heavier built than females. A characteristic belly pouch, called "belly flap", is required between hind legs.

Legs

Medium long, the legs have moderate boning and strong musculature. When standing, the Mau has a characteristic "tiptoe" stance, with hind legs longer than the front.

Feet

Small and delicate, the feet are slightly oval, almost round.

Tail

Medium, the tail is quite thick at base and slightly tapering to the tip.

Coat and texture

Short, the coat should be long enough for each hair (in ticked areas) to carry four alternate light and dark bands, called ticking. It is closelying. In silver and bronze Mau, it is soft and resilient to the touch whereas the black smoke has finer and silky fur.

Patterns

Spotted tabby is the only pattern allowed. There should be a clear contrast between pale ground color and deeper colored markings. The forehead has the characteristic "M" of the tabby pattern, and the eye the typical Egyptian Mascara line.

Colors

Silver
Silver, brilliant, ground color contrasting with black spots. The back of the ears is grayish-pink and tipped in black. Nose, lips and eyes are outlined in black. Throat, chin and nostrils are silver, appearing white. Nose leather is brick red. Paw pads are black with black around the toes and back feet.

Bronze
Bronze, luminous ground color, fading from tawny buff to ivory on underside, darker on rump and contrasting with black or dark brown spots.

Grey undercoat is accepted. Back of ear is tawny pink tipped in dark brown to black. Throat, chin and nostrils range from off-white to beige. Nose leather is brick red. Paw pads are dark brown to black with same color between toes and at the back of hind legs.

Black smoke
Although non agouti, black smoke color on the Egyptian Mau should have enough contrast to make a well-defined spotted tabby pattern plainly visible (ghost markings). The undercolor is luminous silver on ¼ of hair length, the remaining ¾ being charcoal grey. The markings on three quarters of the coat are black, in contrast with the rest of the coat. Throat, chin and nostrils are lighter in color. Nose, lips and eyes are outlined in black. Nose leather and paw pads are black with black around the toes and at the back of hind legs.

Black
Although non agouti, black color on the Egyptian Mau should have enough contrast to make the spotted tabby pattern (ghost markings) visible. The coat is shiny all over.

Allowances

Amber colored eyes under 2 years of age.

Penalize

Round or short head.
Pointed muzzle.
Small ears.
Round, small or oriental eyes.
Cobby or oriental body.
Short tail.
Spots touching each other on the body.
Several tarnish traces in silver.
Lack of broken necklace.

Withhold all awards

Lack of spots.
Wrong eye color.
White locket or spots.
Pattern other than spotted.
Rosettes.
Lack of ticking in silver or bronze.
Glitter.
Red coloring in bronze, overall tarnish in silver.
General show penalties and withholdings.

Points

<u>Head (30 points)</u>
    Shape   5
    Muzzle   5
    Eyes (shape and color)   15
    Ears = 5

<u>Body (30 points)</u>
    Torso   15
    Legs   5
    Feet   5
    Tail   5

<u>Coat and texture (40 points)</u>
    Length and texture   5

Pattern 20
Color 15

THE MAU TEMPER

The temper of the cat varies from one individual to another, just the same as for his human friends. However, characteristic traits of the breed can be identified.

A gluey temper

The Egyptian mau is often qualified as a cat-dog. It is really sticky, does not hesitate following you wherever you go in the house during house works.

Breakfast is a very interesting activity: after a long night, at last you are available for the so much longed endearment session. This adorable Mau cat will then climb on your knees and will rub against your arm which, at the same time, will desperately be trying to control the path described by your cup of nice hot coffee!

Very discreet

On evening, while watching TV, you will suddenly realize that it is there lying and dozing on your knees without your knowing it!

Expressive

Often, it looks at you and its eyes it can transmit many messages. It does not mew too noisily, but modulates its voice and is able to express many things.

Sometimes bashful

Some progenies are shyer than others. These shy cats have a tendency to run away from those they do not recognize as members of the family. They are often cats belonging to one person only. When a visitor is present, they move to another room or hide under a piece of furniture. They are no attracted by vast spaces: they prefer a reassuring small home.

It is during the quietness of the evening that even the most timid of them come and lie on the bed and finally get their caresses they are so keen on.

These ~~ones~~ are not there for attracting the admiration of visitors. They are there for giving ~~a~~ true affection to the master who deserves it.

Often gluttonous

Compared to the Abyssinian, the Mau is a quite calm cat in the kitchen!

Let's be fair: they are not all greedy; but a good part of them, which cannot be ignored, is really interested in what is going on there and is keen to run some risks to improve their everyday meal.

I know one who is ready to slip his paw under the kitchen knife to grab a piece of meat (Vishnu!). Another faces the wrath of the dogs (King Charles: no danger, but the cat doesn't know) in trying to steal their food. And when it is the rich food of kittens, it is delirious.

Really, some days I must close the door to remain alone in the kitchen!

A speedy cat

It is not a fuzz-ball! When playing or trying to escape from you (no, mum, you will not give me my medicines!), he is almost impossible to be seized.

Under its belly, there is a piece of skin hanging down, the belly pouch or belly flap. This pouch allows the cat to lengthen better when running or jumping. In this way, it can jump over more than two meters or run at more than 50 km/h! Well, not all of them: when the pouch is quite full, the cat loses its agility (any allusion to our lovely Fleur would be purely coincidental)…

A strong personality

Whether it is very tender, a little shy or semi-savage (like those living free in Egypt), the Mau has a very strong personality. A relationship mixing affection and respect settles between the two of you. Impossible to ignore him or his desires.

The Mau, when in need of caresses will not stop until it gets them (I saw you, Tiw).

This Mau requiring ~~the~~ respect for its tranquility, will be able to convince you that you have the right to get close, talk, have a personalized approach but do not have the right to touch it and it will assume an indignant countenance if the status quo is not respected.

Concerning the one who has chosen to love you above everyone else, when the time of hated corporal cares comes, it will wriggle, scream, show it could defend itself... and will avoid causing any harm to you!

There is also the little savage born in Egypt which has adopted you. Its presence and affection are such that you have to exert an effort to keep in mind you cannot hold it in your arms.

Finally, there is Pharaoh, the wise one: its personality is a relaxing one. It lies alongside cats, dogs and humans and also calms down ~~also~~ the most excited of them.

The cat is already known for being an animal with a strongly expressive personality. This is remarkably true of the Mau.

SOME EGYPTIAN MAUS

For pronunciation, remember that w is a vowel which sounds like "ou" in the word "you".

CH = Champion
CI = international Champion
GCI = International Grand Champion
CE = European Champion
GCE = European Grand Champion
GC = Grand Champion (CFA)

PR = Premior
PI = International Premior
GPI = International Grand Premior
PE = European Premior
GPE = European Grand Premior
GP = Grand Premior (CFA)

Vasar

CE VASAR

Born March 21, 1995 of EC Pazlo Friend O'mr Cairo and Sangpur of Fagitta of de Joha
European Champion

Vasar is a worthy representative of the cattery du Nil Blanc, Dianick Masson, Switzerland.

This is his photo in Atout Chat Magazine, which made French cat fanciers anxious to know and own this breed. And it is Vasar's children who initiated the creation of the first Mau breedings in France:

> *Elendril du Nil Blanc and Élinor du Nil Blanc, chatterie de Fondcombe*
> *Evora du Nil Blanc, chatterie de Bélénus*

Vasar has been for a long time the mascot of AIME, the International Association for the Egyptian Mau. His picture is on nearly all AIME documents.

Élendril

CE ELENDRIL du Nil Blanc

born July 2, 1997 of CHI Vasar and CHI Balayan von Dracusan
European Champion, several titles of best in show
Best Variety in FIFe world championship in Milan (1999)

When we first met with the beauty of the Egyptian Mau, we could not resist it. We started looking for a little couple. It took great patience considering the scarcity of M aus in Europe at that time. Thus it was that Élendril and Élinor finally joined the family.

Élendril is a male who has had exceptional success on shows and has mounted regularly the podium.

Élendril is above all very affectionate and awfully shy! He is attached only to his family and his family is first of all Kiyasa...

Élendril had a busy breeding career. Since other males were able to take over, Élendril has enjoyed a deserved (and early) retirement: he spends it with Kiyasa at Rose-Marie's who was admitted into the small circle of his intimate friends!

With Élinor du Nil Blanc:
- Pamose de Fondcombe, silver male
- Princesse Nefermeren de Fondcombe, silver female
- Pâkhet de Fondcombe, smoke female
- Peret de Fondcombe, silver female
- Ptah Hotep de Fondcombe, silver male
- Ptolémée de Fondcombe, silver male

With Mas-Ree Maus Osiris:
- Sunrise Abycats Pacha, silver male
- Sunrise Abycats Pharaon, silver male
- Sunrise Abycats Philae, silver female
- Sunrise Abycats Pi-Lazuli, silver female
- Sunrise Abycats Psyché, silver female

With Nisis du Vieux-Pont:
- Phoenix d'Illos, silver male
- Psam d'Illos, silver male
- Philae d'Illos, silver female

With Tavaron Kiyasa:
- Pashedu de Fondcombe, silver male

Sen-sen

GCE, GC-RW Brockhaven SEN-SEN of Fondcombe

born March 24, 1999 of GC Tavaron Maumeo of Brockhaven and GC, RW Brockhaven Osira
U.S. Grand Champion, Regional Winner - European Grand Champion 1st or 2nd in all Mau specials which he attended in France and Europe

Sen-sen was specially selected by Dot Brocksom to enable breeders to have a high quality sire. When Sen-sen arrived in France, he had already been Grand Champion of the United States. He has by now reached the peak of his career in Europe, too.

Upon his arrival after a very long journey, and being already 15 months old, Sen-Sen proved a very, very cuddly cat immediately and took possession of the house without qualms and without particular reaction towards the many cats and dogs with whom he was going to live from then on...

Sen-sen is a model of tenderness and balance: not only is he wonderfully beautiful, but he is also extremely sweet. When he perches around your neck, he retracts his claws carefully. The hug is all the better. He is also very talkative! He is a true Lord.

Okay, nobody is perfect: He cannot stand other sires near him...

With Fleur du Nil Blanc:
- ➤ *Re-Shaï de Fondcombe, silver male*
- ➤ *Renepou de Fondcombe, silver female*
- ➤ *Resout de Fondcombe, silver female*

With Mas-Ree Maus Osiris:
- ➤ *Sunrise Abycats Schwartz, smoke male*
- ➤ *Sunrise Abycats Speedy, smoke male*

- Sunrise Abycats Sphynx, silver male
- Sunrise Abycats Scarlett, silver female

With Renen de Fondcombe:
- Sat-Imen de Fondcombe, silver female
- Seneket de Fondcombe, silver female
- Sothis de Fondcombe, silver female
- Swt de Fondcombe, silver female

With Tavaron's Sarina:
- Swnet de Fondcombe, silver female
- Sechen de Fondcombe, silver female

With Brockhaven Dot's Heart of Fondcombe:
- Tep-Hery de Fondcombe, silver male

With Resout de Fondcombe:
- Tep de Fondcombe, silver male
- Tanis de Fondcombe, silver female
- Tit de Fondcombe, silver female

With Tavaron's Nout of Fondcombe:
- Timna de Fondcombe, silver male
- Twt de Fondcombe, silver female

With Senet de Fondcombe:
- Uppity de Fondcombe, silver male
- Upchange de Fondcombe, bronze female

Anwar and Pharaoh

PR (CFA), GPI Brockhaven Anwar of Fondcombe   GC, GPI Brockhaven Pharaoh of Fondcombe

Both born July 4, 2000 at Dorothea Brocksom, United States.
Anwar was born of GC Tavaron Maumeo of Brockhaven and GC, RW Brockhaven Osira (so he is one of Sen-sen's brothers)
Pharaoh was born ofGC Brockhaven Mamnoonam and Brockhaven Philomene, DM

Purchased by two Swiss brothers, they flew to their new families. Unfortunately, stopovers, delays and formalities made the journey particularly long and tiring. So, upon arrival they were in a hurry to let off steam a bit and to satisfy their physiological needs.

Indignant about such behavior, their unworthy host families warned that such monsters had no place at their homes! So we adopted them and are all the happier for it. Models of equilibrium, trust and tenderness they agree perfectly well with all our canine and feline small world. They are often huddled against each other, and quickly found the path to our bed, like all the others!

Sahourê

born December 3, 1998 in Egypt, recognized as Egyptian Mau in 1999

Virtually all breeding Maus descend from the first three subjects imported in 1956 to the U.S. by Princess Troubetzkoi. We are thus confronted with inbreeding problems. Therefore we conducted extensive research to find a new subject in the country of origin of the breed.

Sahourê was born in an Egyptian family. It has been acclimatized to domestic life. He is a very sociable and lovable cat with humans.

By contrast, he is really very domineering with other cats. He supports only the presence of females...

He also has a strong character: if he says no, it is difficult to force him. At the vet's, even 5 persons are not enough to hold him motionless...

Having smoke and bronze genes, he transmitted all the colors of the Mau with our females: silver, bronze, smoke, and even black.

Two of the kittens he had with Élinor took root in the United States. Sahourê is also the father of Renen and Senefer who in turn produced magnificent lineages.

Sahourê brought not only new blood into the breed, but his babies are very beautiful, tender character and... hilarious! What luck!

With Élinor du Nil Blanc:
- *Resou de Fondcombe, bronze male*
- *Rechout de Fondcombe, silver female*
- *Reqeh de Fondcombe, silver female*
- *Renen de Fondcombe, silver female*

With Brockhaven Dot's Heart of Fondcombe:
- *Senefer de Fondcombe, silver male*
- *Sat de Fondcombe, silver female blotched*
- *Sefet de Fondcombe, bronze female*
- *Swn de Fondcombe, bronze female*

With Tavaron's Nout of Fondcombe:
- *Rahes-Re de Fondcombe, bronze male*
- *Reneb de Fondcombe, bronze male*
- *Semer de Fondcombe, bronze male*
- *Senet de Fondcombe, bronze female*

Khâlifa

Born January 1st, 2001 in Egypt

In spring 2001, we were presented in Cairo with a tiny kitten who scratched as much as possible at the woman who / was holding her. After cuddling her we decided not to: take her to France considering the defects she had, especially her white fur and red blinks! But she had other plans: having escaped from her owner, she followed us and we found her installed on the rear axle of our taxi, and she cried heartbreakingly when we started off. What were we to do?

She had chosen us, so she had won her plane ticket! Immediately, a veterinary visit, then a rush to Sami's to buy her everything needed. Once at our hotel: bath, deworming, pest control, oral antibiotics for her wounds, she accepted everything without flinching... and immediately realized that the place of her choice was to be our bed.

Of course she was spayed at 6 months old because her "defects" prevented her from reproducing with our Maus.

This is the story of a thunderbolt, and of an unconditional and immediate trust that has never wavered. Her gaze is exceptionally intense, she speaks to us and takes our hand when asking for hugs, her eyes are so expressive, in short, she is irresistible. Sometimes she is called "Khalifa mad with love."

Otta

Born in Egypt

Fourth expedition to Egypt to find new blood. Until then, we have brought home Sahourê and Khalifa (not for reproduction). This time we are lucky: under a fishmonger's stall, among a bunch of cats trying to feast on mouth-watering waste: a cat that looks entirely like the one we are after. Assistance from the butcher helps us to catch this quite uncooperative cat. In modern Egypian, otta means (female) cat: This will be her name.

Shortly after her arrival in France, we realize Otta is pregnant with three beautiful kittens of an unknown father. They will find a host family as house cats.

The presence of white spots on Otta's coat and her kittens make her unsuitable for breeding. But she feels better here than out in the streets, to be sure. Just look at her rounding waist!

Otta has remained a wild child: she cannot bear the slightest attempt to touch her. In this case, she spits, but never shows aggressivity. With great patience, she has become accustomed to us, no longer worries about our proximity, and sometimes we even talk to each other. We believe that denial of contact has become a form of play... Now she looks at us with an air of "you wouldn't dare touch me, would you?" She can be approached to within 5 centimeters, but not be touched!

With a handsome unknown Egyptian
- *Totem de Fondcombe, bronze male*
- *Titus de Fondcombe, bronze male*

> *Tabou de Fondcombe, black male*

Totem, however, remained at home after the departure of his brothers. He seems to have understood what visits were for. So, on visit days, no way to approach him! His vow to stay with us has been fulfilled.

Maslama

born September 1, 2001 in Egypt, recognized as Egyptian Mau in 2003

Maslama was found on the same expedition that helped us find Otta. Almost all our things were packed up and we were having a last trip through the streets of Cairo when we saw a cat looking like a Mau. A little farther on, a little kitten of the same color took refuge in a tree... So let us say that this kitten is Maslama!

Maslama is truly a magnificent bronze: *The epitome of hot: a warm bronze Mau without rufus.*

Having never been manipulated by human hands in his infancy, Maslama has remained a shy cat, without an ounce of aggressivity, which took time to adapt to... our bed and our hugs!

His shyness prevents him from being put on show, but he feels well at home. Luckily, there he is a beaming creature!

With time, his startled glance turned into a surprised glance. With patience and gentleness, he even accepts cuddles!

With Senet de Fondcombe:
> *Upswing de Fondcombe, bronze male*
> *Ba de Fondcombe, black male*
> *Bsw de Fondcombe, black male*

- Upper Egypt de Fondcombe, bronze female
- Bat de Fondcombe, black female

With Tavaron's Sarina of Fondcombe:
- Ulysse de Fondcombe, smoke male
- Uranus de Fondcombe, silver male
- Ubu de Fondcombe, smoke male

With Senekkw de Bélénus:
- Ulhsane de Fondcombe, silver female
- Ursule de Fondcombe, silver female

With Tavaron's Sarina of Fondcombe:
- Vidocq de Fondcombe, silver male
- Valmiki de Fondcombe, silver male
- Velleda de Fondcombe, silver female

Élinor

CHI ELINOR du Nil Blanc

born June 2, 1997 of CHI Vasar and CHI Cleopatra de Joha
International Champion

Elinor is the charming lady who accompanied Élendril to France to start a lineage there and build the reputation of Maus in this country.

Elinor is nicknamed Cocolle (glue-glue). Sometimes, we cannot walk inside the house without being followed by her wherever we go! All is harmonious in her character to such an extent indeed that there is finally nothing more to say.

Her coat is slightly dark, which is penalizing at shows, so she attended only afew. But mated with Élendril, she gave her kittens a very interesting contrasted coat. She also gave birth to Pakhet, a small black smoke female that has made this uncommon color better known.

With Sahourê, a male imported directly from Egypt, she has created a new lineage, a very interesting one to fight against inbreeding. Two of her kittens reside in the United States.

With Élendril du Nil Blanc:
- *Pamose de Fondcombe, silver male*
- *Princesse Nefermeren de Fondcombe, silver female*
- *Pâkhet de Fondcombe, smoke female*
- *Peret de Fondcombe, silver female*
- *Ptah Hotep de Fondcombe, silver male*
- *Ptolémée de Fondcombe, silver male*

With Sahourê:
- *Resou de Fondcombe, bronze male*
- *Rechout de Fondcombe, silver female*
- *Reqeh de Fondcombe, silver female*
- *Renen de Fondcombe, silver female*

Fleur

Fleur du Nil Blanc

born April 16, 1998 of CHI Darwin and CHI Balayan von Dracusan several titles as best in show kitten.

After Élendril and Elinor, we wanted a second female. Dianick told us she had a very promising young female... As soon as we put her next to Élendril (which is really beautiful), we found she was beautifully contrasted. At shows, she was voted best variety and best kitten (6-10 months).

Fleur has a golden character. She is also glue-like. More importantly, she is gluttonous. So much so that she had to interrupt her show career due to a well marked obesity. Whenever we thought she was pregnant, it was only obesity. When she at last became really pregnant, we realized it very late... Putting her on a diet makes her unhappy, to such a point that she becomes dirty to show her displeasure!

She feels great affection for our King Charles dog, Nais, and suckled her for years, sometimes enough to cause milk surges. His daughter Resout inherited her taste for Nais, but not her obesity.

With Brockhaven Sen-sen of Fondcombe:
- *Re-Shaï de Fondcombe, silver male*
- *Renepou de Fondcombe, silver female*
- *Resout de Fondcombe, silver female*

Kiyasa

Tavaron's KIYASA

born March 18, 1998 United States of GC Triangle Mau Asparet of Tavaron and Brockhaven JAID of Tavaron, at Rebecca and Stephen Bergeron's home

After our first Maus from Switzerland, we wanted to diversify our lines. We selected Kiyasa at Becky and Steve's in the U.S. How difficult it is to choose from afar! The choice was good, however: Kiyasa is really beautiful and a very pleasant character. She is not at all out of place in our little Mau family.

She arrived alone by air. But in top form and full of tenderness. She immediately adapted to her new home (it seems to be a common trait in Maus, doesn't it?) and to the whole family. Since then she has proved a very tender cat, both a gourmet and a scoundrel.

By contrastshe has not proven to be a good mother, so we decided to stop breeding her. Along with her inseparable companion, Élendril, she tastes the joys of early retirement on the Riviera.

When our American friends, Becki and Steve, heard of this early retirement, they presented us with her sister Sarina, a marvelous gift, so that we can still work with this beautiful line.

With Élendril du Nil Blanc:
- *Pashedu de Fondcombe, silver male*

Pakhet

Pakhet de Fondcombe

born March 16, 1999 of GCHI Élendril du Nil Blanc and CHI Élinor du Nil Blanc.

Pakhet is one of the kittens of the first Egyptian Mau litter born in our home. Unexpectedly (I have learned feline genetics since then...), there was a little black smoke baby among them. It was Pakhet. She is a very lively little rascal who knows how to show all her companions the kind of kitten she is!

Pakhet contributed to making that odd color known and appreciated. Some even say it is the favorite color of sophisticated fanciers.

Nout

CHI Tavaron's NOUT of Fondcombe

born May 20, 1999 of Sangpur Blackthing Badaging of Tavaron and GC Brockhaven Sarobbie of Tavaron
International Champion

For Sahourê, we wanted a beautiful bronze female, hence the arrival of Nout.

Not only is she beautiful but she is very affectionate and very attached to us. She is even more gluey than Elinor! When she is called, she comes along as quickly as a dog.

Of course, the first thing she found on arriving was the bed. She took a few days to tolerate our King Charles lying together with her on the bed.

Her main drawback: an immoderate love for phone cords...

Now neutered, Nout, who clearly prefers to live in a small group, shares the hugs of her new master, Philip, only with her boyfriend H, a neutered Bengal.

With Sahourê:
- *Rahes-Re de Fondcombe, bronze male*
- *Reneb de Fondcombe, bronze male*
- *Semer de Fondcombe, bronze male*
- *Senet de Fondcombe, bronze female*

With Brockhaven Sen-sen of Fondcombe:
- *Timna de Fondcombe, silver male*
- *Twt de Fondcombe, silver female*

Dot's Heart

Brockhaven DOT'S HEART

born May 25, 1999 of GC Brockhaven Mamnoomam and DM Brockhaven Philomene

Our American friend Dot Brocksom kept this lovely little Silver cat for us. Her spots are unusually well marked! On her right shoulder, she has a mark / looking like a pretty little heart, hence her name.

Dot's Heart has always been a little shy. Moreover, she transmitted this trait to her son Senefer.

Yet, when Nicolas and Brigitte came to visit our cattery, it was love at first sight: that pussy who feared all visitors, huddled in the arms of Brigitte and therefore left with: her and Nicolas. Now she is the joy of the owners of the "Hôtel du Cygne".

With Sahourê:
- *Senefer de Fondcombe, silver male*
- *Sat de Fondcombe, silver female blotched*
- *Sefet de Fondcombe, bronze female*
- *Swn de Fondcombe, bronze female*

With Brockhaven Sen-sen of Fondcombe:
- *Tep-Hery de Fondcombe, silver male*

Renen

RENEN de Fondcombe

born July 8, 2000 of Sahourê de Fondcombe and CHI Élinor du Nil Blanc

The first litter of Sahourê, our male imported directly from Egypt!

Her brother Resou (bronze) and her sister Rechout (Silver) live in the United States where, hopefully, they will create new lines. Upon arrival, they participated in CFA shows, were chosen for finals and won some Bests. No doubt about it: they please!

What has most excited our friends American breeders is their size: at 4 months old, they are as big as 8 month kittens. Beautiful, strong and from a new line, they will find a place for themselves in breeding programs in the United States and Europe.

Renen has a strong character and is not so soft with other cats. So, after handing over to her daughters, she took a well-deserved cuddly retirement, far away from all those other felines!

With Brockhaven Sen-sen of Fondcombe:

- Sat-Imen de Fondcombe, silver female
- Seneket de Fondcombe, silver female
- Sothis de Fondcombe, silver female
- Swt de Fondcombe, silver female

Sarina

GCE, CH (CFA) Tavaron's SARINA of Fondcombe

born March 14, 2000 in United States of GC Triangle Mau Asparet of Tavaron and Jaid Brockhaven of Tavaron, belonging to Rebecca and Stephen Bergeron

U.S. Champion, Grand Champion of Europe

Tavaron's Kiyasa was not a good mother, so we decided not to mate her again. When our American friends Becki and Steve learned it, they gave us her sister Sarina so that we can still work with this very nice line. This gift is all the more extraordinary because Sarina was the favorite of Steve.

Sarina is not only very elegant, but she also has a lovely character. A purring pot of glue! Sarina and Sen-sen are the most outstanding representatives of the Egyptian Mau: both extremely beautiful with a golden character. Precious lineages!

This perfectly balanced character is reflected in her children. Hopefully, there will be many of them.

With Brockhaven Sen-sen of Fondcombe:
- ➢ *Swnet de Fondcombe, silver female*
- ➢ *Sechen de Fondcombe, silver female*

With Senefer de Fondcombe:
- ➢ *Tep-Nefer de Fondcombe, silver male*
- ➢ *Tiw de Fondcombe, silver female*

With Maslama:
- ➢ *Ulysse de Fondcombe, smoke male*
- ➢ *Uranus de Fondcombe, silver male*
- ➢ *Ubu de Fondcombe, smoke male*

With Maslama:
- ➢ *Vidocq de Fondcombe, silver male*
- ➢ *Valmiki de Fondcombe, silver male*
- ➢ *Velleda de Fondcombe, silver female*

Resout

RESOUT de Fondcombe

born September 5, 2000 of Brockhaven Sen-Sen of Fondcombe and Fleur du Nil Blanc

A little treasure which has inherited the calm of her mother and the fabulous love of her dad. She chose to spend most of her time on our bed.

With Brockhaven Sen-sen of Fondcombe:
- Tep de Fondcombe, silver male
- Tanis de Fondcombe, silver female
- Tit de Fondcombe, silver female

Here, let us note a line originating from her dad! The villains were very discreet! Children have Sen-sen's golden character.

Marie-Chantal

GCE SENEKKW de Bélénus (prononcer Sénékou)

born February 3, 2001 of Faustine du Nil Blanc and CH Danton du Nil Blanc

European Grand Champion

Since the departure of Pakhet, we have had no more black smoke Mau at home. This rare color has a special charm. Fortunately, a pretty girl was born in Nantes, at Philip and Sandrine's home! Besides her wonderful color, Senekkw de Bélénus has a golden character. Having been bred in a family - and with dogs - she has adapted smoothly. She is extremely tender and follows us around like a puppy. A note: her formidable appetite! Only Khalifa can compete in gluttony with her.

When she arrived home, she was called Marie-Chantal. Her nickname remained.

With Maslama:
- > *Ulhsane de Fondcombe, silver female*
- > *Ursule de Fondcombe, silver female*

Senefer

CI SENEFER de Fondcombe

born August 15, 2001 of Sahourê de Fondcombe and Brockhaven Dot's Heart of Fondcombe

International Champion. Supreme Best in his first show.

A charming young boy, very elegant, a little reserved but not calling for caresses, who prefers to wait until we're lying in bed to join us there

Senefer offers us an ideal characteristic feature: spots all along the spine.

Often, in silver Maus, makeup under the eyes is expressed by a dark shadow. When the cat closes his eyes, you feel as if two eyes were still glazing at you. With Senefer, this feeling is very strong.

Senefer's shyness and escapades during shows attracted much notice (specialty: hiding below the podium). This trait came from his mother, Dot's Heart, and has not been mitigated by the blood of his father Sahourê.

One day in 2002, Senefer managed to find an escape route and fled, settling a few hundred meters from the house. Despite our best efforts, he never wanted to return. Ever since he has been living in the street where he enjoys full freedom. Even the cold of winter does not seem to bother him.

Unfortunately, in the streets, there are cars! Never let your cat roam outside.

With Tavaron's Sarina of Fondcombe:
- *Tep-Nefer de Fondcombe, silver male*
- *Tiw de Fondcombe, silver female*

Senet

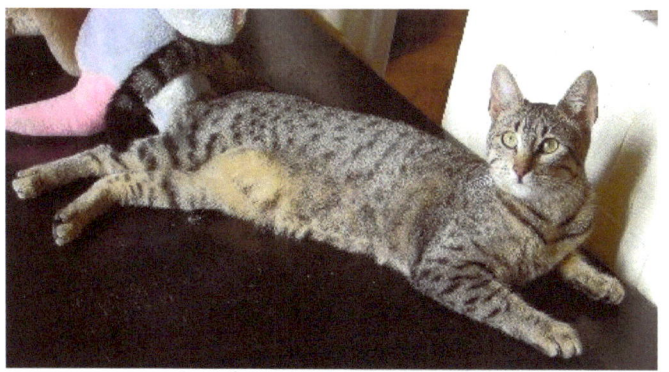

GCI SENET de Fondcombe

born August 12, 2001 of Sahourê de Fondcombe and Tavaron's Nout of Fondcombe
International Grand Champion

A beautiful bronze female rather domineering towards some of her fellow-creatures, even a little feverish with some... However, she feels a passionate love for her boyfriend, Pharaoh. She is delicious with humans.

With Brockhaven Sen-sen of Fondcombe:
- *Uppity de Fondcombe, silver male*
- *Upchange de Fondcombe, bronze female*

With Maslama:
- *Upswing de Fondcombe, bronze male*
- *Ba de Fondcombe, black male*
- *Bsw de Fondcombe, black male*
- *Upper Egypt de Fondcombe, bronze female*
- *Bat de Fondcombe, noire female*

Upswing got a best variety and was nominated for Best in Show at the largest special Mau show at Chinagora (2003). During the same show, Ba seduced everyone with her elegance!

Tiw & Tep-Nefer

TEP-NEFER de Fondcombe

born December 24, 2002 of CE Tavaron's Sarina of Fondcombe and GCHI Senefer de Fondcombe

Before fleeing, Senefer whispered sweet nothings to Sarina. His children have inherited his elegance and the beauty and character of their mother! A precious mixture.

TIW de Fondcombe

Tiw perpetuates the elegance of his father with, thanks to his mother, a shorter and therefore better head.

Tep-Nefer has a striking resemblance to his dad, minus the latter's shyness. Tep-Nefer lives happily with our friend Sandrine, at Bélénus cattery.

Tiw with Uther Pendragon de Fondcombe:
- *Velvet de Fondcombe, silver female*
- *Vivian de Fondcombe, silver female*
- *Viva Voce de Fondcombe, silver female*
- *Vestal Virgin de Fondcombe, silver female*

Bronzie

UP-CHANGE de Fondcombe

born February 12, 2003 of GCHI Senet de Fondcombe and GC, RW, GCHE Brockhaven Sen-sen of Fondcombe.

Sahourê's granddaughter on the maternal side, she has a warmer-coloured coat than her mother's, and she has inherited her father's softer character.

She is the first bronze descendant of Sen-sen. Until then, I had been convinced that Sen-sen didn't carry the bronze gene!

Sothis

SOTHIS de Fondcombe

born June 7, 2001 of GC, RW Brockhaven Sen-Sen of Fondcombe and Renen de Fondcombe

Sefen, Sothis, Swnet and Sechen went through a divorce. Not theirs but that of their breeders. After the divorce, the one who got the Maus was unable to look after them properly and so neglected them... So, members of AIME recovered the cats. The poor things were in a deplorable state: lack of care, undernourished: lacking emotional contact and being depressed (yes, cat depression does exist, and cats may die of it). In addition, Sefen had still fulfilled his duty as a male. Sothis was the only one not to become pregnant in these deplorable conditions.

From her mother Sothis has got a strong character which she shows when she is with other cats, but she is very gentle with humans. Her coat is perfect: not a single stripe on her body!

Swnet

SWNET de Fondcombe

born June 20, 2001 GC, of GC, RW Brockhaven Sen-Sen of Fondcombe and CH Tavaron's Sarina of Fondcombe

Swnet returned from Switzerland at the same time as Sothis. Recovering her health was difficult for her because she was both depressed and pregnant!

Her dream: to find her first home again; her passion: her kitten. With these two ingredients, she recovered her good health.

A huge resemblance with her mother. Her character is worthy of that of her two parents.

SEFEN de Fondcombe

With Sefen de Fondcombe:
- *Uther Pendragon de Fondcombe, silver male*

Uther Pendragon

UTHER PENDRAGON de Fondcombe

born August 15, 2003 of Sefen de Bélénus and Swnet de Fondcombe

Uther, nicknamed Zouzou or Vishnu, is a little bastard who was able very soon to find himself ~~his~~ a place among adults. At two months old, you could see who would be the ruler of the little band. A scoundrel of a cat, both mischievous and playful, he has shown that he is also the best in tenderness and delicacy. His "little dog" side is worthy of the Egyptian Mau's reputation.

Growing up, he became a beautiful and very impressive male. Always hovering around females and kittens. He lives in fairly good agreement with Maslama because the latter, although quiet and reserved, is built to face any possible offence...

Greedy, thieving, glue-like, cuddly: all the faults that we love...

With Tiw de Fondcombe:
- *Velvet de Fondcombe, silver female*
- *Vivian de Fondcombe, silver female*
- *Viva Voce de Fondcombe, silver female*
- *Vestal Virgin de Fondcombe, silver female*

A special mention for Velvet who is even more greedy, thieving, glue-like and affectionate than her father!

Velleda

CH VELLEDA de Fondcombe

Born June 18, 2004 of Maslama of Fondcombe and Tavaron's Sarina of Fondcombe.
U.S. Champion

Curiously, Velleda remained very, very close to her mother Sarina. So, her natural tendency to shyness is expressed. Utimately she feels far better snuggling against Sarina on the lap of mom or dad...

Daughter of Maslama, imported from Egypt, Velleda behaved brilliantly on shows and pretty effortlessly won a CFA championship title. She is evidence that as early as the first generation, we can have very beautiful cats, according to their breed, and that the feline organizations recognize this.

I must say that she offers a really extraordinary contrast!

EGYPTIAN NAMES FOR EGYPTIANS CATS

Egyptian Mau breeding and ancient Egypt research get along well together Thus many of our cats wear Egyptian names. Here are their translation and representation in hieroglyphs.

A I M E

Hieroglyphs can be written from left to right or from right to left.
When hieroglyphs are written from left to right, personages look toward left.
When hieroglyphs are written from right to left, personages look toward right.
Here, we wrote hieroglyphs from left to right.

Thanks to Mark Johns and Mark Millmore for their transcription tool
http://www.eyelid.co.uk/e-name.htm

Note: In France, usage is that all the kittens born during the same year have a name beginning with the same letter. The following year, the next letter of the alphabet is used. Letters K, Q, W, X, Y, Z are not used, so the same letter comes back every 20 years. Some Latin letters are not used in the hieroglyphic alphabet, so there are no ancient Egyptian names during the corresponding years.

For pronunciation, remember that *w* is a vowel which sounds like *ou* in the word *you*.

<u>Beginning with B</u>

Name & Translation	Hieroglyphic
Ba *Soul*	

Name & Translation	Hieroglyphic
Bat *Splendour*	
Bsw *Fire*	

1999 – names beginning with P

Name & Translation	Hieroglyphic
Pâkhet *A cathead goddess*	
Pamose *Pharaoh*	
Pashedu *Artist of Seti period*	

Name & Translation	Hieroglyphic
Peret *Strength*	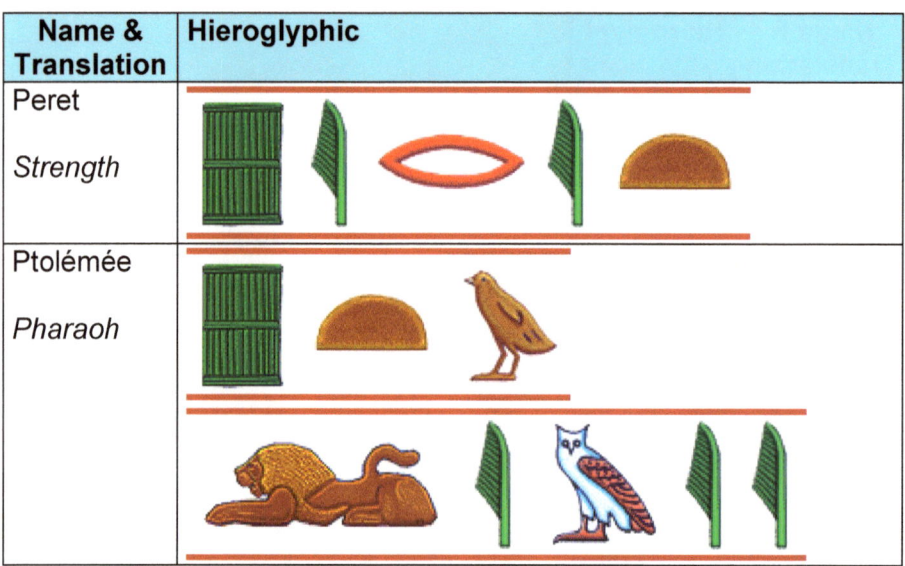
Ptolémée *Pharaoh*	

2000 – *names beginning with R*

Name & Translation	Hieroglyphic
Rahes-re *Winter sun*	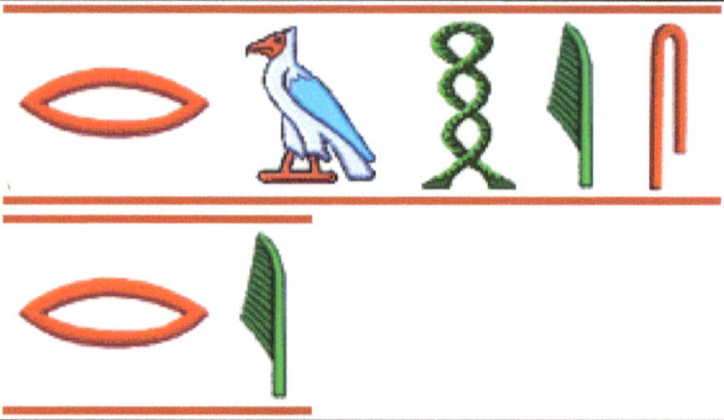
Renen *(baby) rocking*	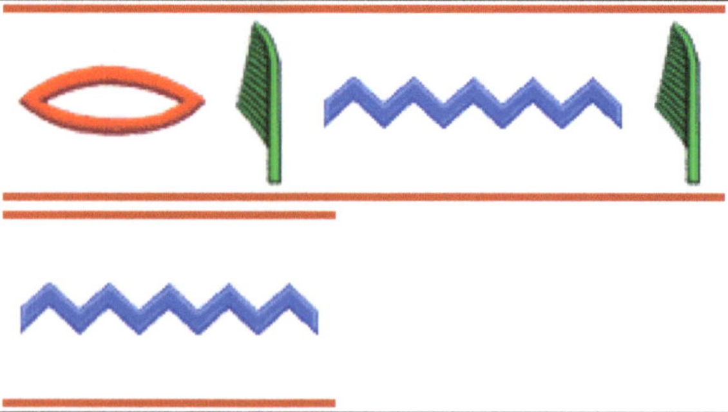

Name & Translation	Hieroglyphic
Renet *Joy*	
Renepou *God of year*	
Re-shaï *God Râ*	
Reshout *Cake*	
Resou *God of south*	

Name & Translation	Hieroglyphic
Resout Reed	

2001 – names beginning with S

Name & Translation	Hieroglyphic
Sahourê Pharaoh	
Sat Bead	
Sat-imen Perfect bead	
Sechen Water lily	

Name & Translation	Hieroglyphic
Sefen *Gentle*	
Sefe *Holy oilt*	
Semer *Beaming*	
Senefer *Pharaoh* Or *Make happy*	
Senekhet *Strengthen*	

Name & Translation	Hieroglyphic
Senekkw — *Darkness*	
Senet — *Lionness goddess*	
Sen-sen — *Friendship*	
Sothis — *Greec name of Sopdet*	
Swnet — *Medicine*	
Swt — *White crown*	

2002 – names beginning with T

Name & Translation	Hieroglyphic
Tanis *Greec name of Djanet*	
Tep *The beginning*	
Tephery *Mouth*	
Tepnefer *Goddess of happyness*	

Name & Translation	Hieroglyphic
Timna	
Tit *Gift*	
Tiw	
Twt *Snake god*	

2003 – names begining with U
No luck: there is no Egyptian word begining by U.

LES STARS DE L'AIME

Within AIME, our cats are our stars. Primarily, because they are <u>our</u> cats, beings we love (our husbands, wives and children know and accept this because none of them is forgotten).

Among them some have attracted special notice. So let's talk a little about them.

1998

<u>CE VASAR</u>

Breeder: Mme PERNIOLA - chatterie de Joha

Owner: Dianick MASSON - chatterie du Nil Blanc

1st AIME European Champion

Vasar is AIME mascot

GC, BW, RW Brockhaven OSIRA

Breeder: Dorothea BROCKSOM - Brockhaven cattery

Owner: Dorothea BROCKSOM - Brockhaven cattery

GC, RW Brockhaven MAFDET

Breeder: Dorothea BROCKSOM - Brockhaven cattery

Owner: Dorothea BROCKSOM - Brockhaven cattery

2nd best of breed CFA 97-98

DM Brockhaven PHILOMENE

Breeder: Dorothea BROCKSOM - Brockhaven cattery

Owner: Dorothea BROCKSOM - Brockhaven cattery

Distinguished Merit CFA

1999

CE ELENDRIL du Nil Blanc

Breeder: Dianick MASSON - chatterie du Nil Blanc

Owner: Didier HALLÉPÉE - Chatterie de Fondcombe

Best Egyptian Mau at FIFe world show in Milan (I)

GC Brockhaven KALAKALA

Breeder: Dorothea BROCKSOM - Brockhaven cattery

Owner: Dorothea BROCKSOM - Brockhaven cattery

2nd best of breed CFA 98-99

2000

<u>SAHOURÊ of Fondcombe</u>

Owner: Didier HALLÉPÉE - Chatterie de Fondcombe

First Egyptian Mau coming from Egypt since the 50's

2001

<u>GC, RW Brockhaven SEN-SEN of Fondcombe</u>

Breeder: Dorothea BROCKSOM - Brockhaven cattery

Owner: Didier HALLÉPÉE - Chatterie de Fondcombe

Best Egyptian Mau at Beldar (B) Special Mau show

2nd best Egyptian Mau at Chinagora 2001 (F) Special Mau show

GC Tavaron's DOTTE COOLPEPPER

Breeder: Steve & Rebecca BERGERON - Tavaron's Cattery

Owner: Steve & Rebecca BERGERON - Tavaron's Cattery

CFA Grand Champion within 2 shows

2002

CHI SENEFER de Fondcombe

Breeder: Didier HALLÉPÉE - Chatterie de Fondcombe

Owner: Didier HALLÉPÉE - Chatterie de Fondcombe

Son of Sahourê of Fondcombe, Supreme Best at his 1st show

<u>CE, GC, RW Brockhaven SEN-SEN of Fondcombe</u>

Photos Christophe Hermeline/Doxicat

Breeder: Dorothea BROCKSOM - Brockhaven cattery

Owner: Didier HALLÉPÉE - Chatterie de Fondcombe

2nd best Egyptian Mau at Chinagora 2002 (F) Special Mau show

<u>GCE IMHOTEP RA-LAIDACH della Dea Sekhmet</u>

Breeder: Barbara ROVELLI - chatterie della Dea Sekhmet

Owner: Christiane SEVAL-CHAPTAL

1st AIME European Grand Champion

2nd best Egyptian Mau and best bronze Egyptian Mau at Chinagora 2002 (F) Special Mau show

<u>CH Imhotep SOBEK</u>

Photo Christophe Hermeline/Doxicat

Breeder: Myriam KHÉRIF - Chatterie Imhotep

Owner: Valérie DELIBES

Best black smoke Egyptian Mau at Chinagora 2002 (F) Special Mau show

<u>GCE Princesse NEFERMEREN de Fondcombe</u>

Photo Christophe Hermeline/Doxicat

Breeder: Didier HALLÉPÉE - Chatterie de Fondcombe

Owner: Christiane GUÉRIN - Chatterie des Horizons de Bastet

1st AIME silver female European Grand Champion

2003

<u>GCE, GC, RW Brockhaven SEN-SEN of Fondcombe</u>

Breeder: Dorothea BROCKSOM - Brockhaven cattery

Owner: Didier HALLÉPÉE - Chatterie de Fondcombe

1st AIME silver male European Grand Champion

<u>CH TWT de Fondcombe</u>

Photo Christophe Hermeline/Doxicat

Breeder: Didier HALLÉPÉE - Chatterie de Fondcombe

Owner: Bernard & Christiane BOUCHER

1st AIME TICA Champion

Imhotep TRIPHAENA CLEOPÂTRA

Breeder: Myriam KHÉRIF - Chatterie Imhotep

Owner: Christiane SEVAL-CHAPTAL

1st black smoke Mau at a Best in show

2004

GCE SENEKKW de Bélénus

Breeder: Sandrine MAISNIER-DUFOUR – Chatterie de Bélénus

Owner: Didier HALLÉPÉE - Chatterie de Fondcombe

1st AIME black smoke female European Grand Champion

UTHER PENDRAGON de Fondcombe

Breeder: Didier HALLÉPÉE - Chatterie de Fondcombe

Owner: Didier HALLÉPÉE - Chatterie de Fondcombe

Best Egyptian Mau at Antony 2004 (F) Special Mau show

UPSWING et UPPER-EGYPT de Fondcombe

Breeder: Didier HALLÉPÉE - Chatterie de Fondcombe

Owner: Marie-Thérèse LEFEVRE

For their achievements at Antony 2004 (F) Special Mau show

GC Tavaron's DOTTE COOLPEPPER

Breeder: Steve & Rebecca BERGERON - Tavaron's Cattery

Owner: Steve & Rebecca BERGERON - Tavaron's Cattery

Star of the film « the cat woman » as « Midnight »

THE SPECIAL MAU SHOWS IN FRANCE

The GIEL began organizing shows in 2001. This organization seeming eminently attractive, AIME held a first spontaneous Mau meeting during the Chinagora show in 2001. 18 Maus were gathered on this occasion.

Things having clicked right away, the first French special Mau show was organized in Chinagora in 2002.

In early 2003, the second French special Mau show was hosted in Aubevoye.

Since then, other special Mau shows have been organized.

Chinagora show 2001

On October 13 and 14, 2001, for the first time in France 18 Egyptian Maus were presented at one and the same a show. They got a resounding success.

Attending cats - Silver

Cat	class	Owner	Breeder	Sire / Dam
CH DANTON du Nil Blanc	CACIB M 01/08/96	Sandrine MAISNIER-DUFOUR	Diannick MASSON	CH CHEOPS de Joha Venezia
Tavaron SINOUHE of Bélénus	CAC M 29/07/00	Sandrine MAISNIER-DUFOUR	Steve & Rebecca BERGERON	Sangpur BLACK THING BADAJING CH Tavaron RAIN DROP
Brockhaven SEN-SEN of Fondcombe	CAC M 24/03/99	Marie-Christine HALLÉPÉE	Dorothea BROCKSOM	US GC Tavaron MAUMEO of Brockhaven RW-GC Brockhaven US OSIRA
Matiki's PHOEBE of Wadi Sana'a	CAC F 24/03/99	Guillaume LE BRICON	Yan & Bonnie WIDROW	Ocali SPOTS OF THE DICE of Matiki New Kingdom NINI of Matiki
EVORA du Nil Blanc	CAC F 02/06/97	Sandrine MAISNIER-DUFOUR	Diannick MASSON	CHI VASAR CHI BALAYANA von Dracusan
US CH Tavaron SARINA of Fondcombe	CAC F 14/03/00	Marie-Christine HALLÉPÉE	Steve & Rebecca BERGERON	US GC Triangle ASPARET Mau of Tavaron Brockhaven JAID of Tavaron
REQUEM de Fondcombe	CAC M 08/07/00	Michel GRUNBERG	Marie-Christine HALLÉPÉE	SAHOURÊ of Fondcombe ELINOR du Nil Blanc
RENEPOU de Fondcombe (FLORE)	CAP F Neuter 05/09/00	Catherine FENDER	Marie-Christine HALLÉPÉE	US RW-GC Brockhaven SEN-SEN of Fondcombe FLEUR du Nil Blanc
SECHEN de Fondcombe	3/6 months M 20/06/01	Marie-Christine HALLÉPÉE	Marie-Christine HALLÉPÉE	US RW-GC Brockhaven SEN-SEN of Fondcombe US CH SARINA de Fondcombe
SENEKET de Fondcombe	3/6 months F 09/06/01	Marie-Christine HALLÉPÉE	Marie-Christine HALLÉPÉE	US RW-GC Brockhaven SEN-SEN of Fondcombe RENEN de Fondcombe

Cat	class	Owner	Breeder	Sire / Dam
SWT de Fondcombe	3/6 months F 09/06/01	Marie-Christine HALLÉPÉE	Marie-Christine HALLÉPÉE	US RW-GC Brockhaven SEN-SEN of Fondcombe RENEN de Fondcombe
SARET de Bélénus	3/6 months F 05/05/01	Sandrine MAISNIER-DUFOUR	Sandrine MAISNIER-DUFOUR	CH DANTON du Nil Blanc EVORA du Nil Blanc
SAROS Wadi Sana'a	6/9 months M 26/02/01	Patrice DESGRANGES	Guillaume LE BRICON	SIR ORLANDO von King of Cats Matiki's PHOEBE of Wadi Sana'a
IOUNYT von Skarrabäus	6/9 months F 24/03/01	Myriam KHÉRIF	Sylvia HODEL	De Joha SESOSTRIS CESARE GAHJA von Dracusan
PHILLAE s'Illos	HC F 26/09/99	Christa ARBES	Christa ARBES	CHE Elendril du Nil Blanc NISIS du Vieux Pont

Attending cats - Black Smoke

Cat	class	Owner	Breeder	Sire / Dam
SENEKKW de Bélénus	6/9 months F 03/02/01	Marie-Christine HALLÉPÉE	Sandrine MAISNIER-DUFOUR	CH DANTON du Nil Blanc FAUSTINE du Nil Blanc

Attending cats - Bronze

Cat	class	Owner	Breeder	Sire / Dam
CHI IMHOTEP RA-LAIDACH della Dea Sekhmet	CAGCI M 18/03/00	Christianne SEVAL-CHAPTAL	Massimiliano ROVELLI	CHI HORUS de Joha CHI ESET vom Margelacker
CH Tavaron NOUT of Fondcombe	CACIB F 12/08/01	Marie-Christine HALLÉPÉE	Steve & Rebecca BERGERON	Sangpur BLACK THING BADAJING US GC Brockhaven SAROBBIE of Tavaron
HEKET della Dea Sekhmet	CAC F 18/03/00	Joëlle CHARIER	Massimiliano ROVELLI	CHI HORUS de Joha CHI ESET vom vom Margelacker

October 13

**Best variety
Brockhaven Sen-Sen of Fondcombe**

**Best in show kittens 3-6 month female
Swt de Fondcombe**

October 14: Short hair:

**Best variety
Iounyt von Skarrabäus**

**Best in show kittens 3-6 months female
Swt de Fondcombe**

**Best in show kittens 6-9 months female
Iounyt von Skarrabäus**

**Best of Best
Iounyt von Skarrabäus**

Special Mau, Chinagora 2002

Photo Christophe Hermeline/Doxicat

Attending cats - Silver

Cat	class	Owner	Breeder	Sire / Dam
CHE Brockhaven SEN-SEN of Fondcombe	CAGCE M 24/03/99	Marie-Christine HALLÉPÉE	Dorothea BROCKSOM	US GC Tavaron MAUMEO of Brockhaven RW-GC Brockhaven US OSIRA
CHE PRINCESSE NEFERMEREN de Fondcombe	CAGCE F 16/03/99	Christiane GUÉRIN	Marie-Christine HALLÉPÉE	CHE ÉLENDRIL du Nil Blanc CHI ÉLINOR du Nil Blanc
GCHI IOUNYT von Skarrabäus	CACE F 24/03/01	Myriam KHÉRIF	Sylvia HODEL	De Joha SESOSTRIS CESARE GAHJA von Dracusan
GCHI PI-LAZULI Mau Sunrise Abycats	CACE F 15/08/99	Myriam KHÉRIF	Liliane Rudel	CHE ÉLENDRIL du Nil Blanc Mas-Ree Maus OSIRIS
GCHI Tavaron SARINA of Fondcombe	CACE F 14/03/00	Marie-Christine HALLÉPÉE	Steve & Rebecca BERGERON	US GC Triangle ASPARET Mau of Tavaron Brockhaven JAID of Tavaron
CHI SENEFER de Fondcombe	CAGCI M 15/08/01	Marie-Christine HALLÉPÉE	Marie-Christine HALLÉPÉE	SAHOURÊ of Fondcombe Brockhaven DOT'S HEART of Fobndombe
CH SWT de Fondcombe	CACIB F 09/06/01	Christianne SEVAL-CHAPTAL	Marie-Christine HALLÉPÉE	US RW-GC Brockhaven SEN-SEN of Fondcombe RENEN de Fondcombe

Cat	class	Owner	Breeder	Sire / Dam
RE-SHAÏ de Fondcombe	CAC M 05/09/00	Chantal POISSON-PIOTROWSKI	Marie-Christine HALLÉPÉE	US RW-GC Brockhaven SEN-SEN of Fondcombe Fleur du Nil Blanc
TEP-HERY de Fondcombe	CAC M 06/03/02	Sandy DEVINOY	Marie-Christine HALLÉPÉE	US RW-GC Brockhaven SEN-SEN of Fondcombe Brockhaven DOT'S HEART of Fobndombe
Imhotep SAKKARAH	CAC F 06/09/01	Nadine CHAMPETIER	Myriam KHÉRIF	Imhotep della Dea Sekhmet PI-LAZULI Sunrise Abycats
RESOUT de Fondcombe	CAC F 05/09/00	Marie-Christine HALLÉPÉE	Marie-Christine HALLÉPÉE	US RW-GC Brockhaven SEN-SEN of Fondcombe FLEUR du Nil Blanc
GC Brockhaven PHARAOH of Fondcombe	CAP M Neuter 04/07/00	Marie-Christine HALLÉPÉE	Dorothea BROCKSOM	US GC Brockhaven MAMNOONAM DM-CH Brockhaven PHILOMENE
KHNOUMSES von Skarrabäus	3/6 months M 11/07/02	Myriam KHÉRIF	Silvia HODEL	CE GERONIMO von Skarrabäus IDIS CLEA von Skarrabäus
Imhotep TANAKA	3/6 months F 29/06/02	Myriam KHÉRIF	Myriam KHÉRIF	Sunrise Abycats SPEEDY CHI IOUNYT von Skarrabäus
Imhotep TAOURET	3/6 months F 29/06/02	Myriam KHÉRIF	Myriam KHÉRIF	Sunrise Abycats SPEEDY CHI IOUNYT von Skarrabäus
Imhotep TRYPHAENA-CLEOPATRA	3/6 months F 29/06/02	Christiane SEVAL-CHEPTAL	Myriam KHÉRIF	Sunrise Abycats SPEEDY CHI IOUNYT von Skarrabäus
THÔT de Boutigny	6/9 months M 08/04/02	Michel JOB	Annia STEPNIAK-BOUTIGNY	PTAH-HOTEP de Fondcombe RÊVE of Sweetness
TEP de Fondcombe	6/9 months M Neutre 07/03/02	Zoran RADOVANOVIC	Marie-Christine HALLÉPÉE	US RW-GC Brockhaven SEN-SEN of Fondcombe RESOUT de Fondcombe
TIT de Fondcombe	6/9 months F 07/03/02	Marie-Christine HALLÉPÉE	Marie-Christine HALLÉPÉE	US RW-GC Brockhaven SEN-SEN of Fondcombe RESOUT de Fondcombe
TANIS de Fondcombe	6/9 months F 07/03/02	Michel JOB	Marie-Christine HALLÉPÉE	US RW-GC Brockhaven SEN-SEN of Fondcombe RESOUT de Fondcombe
TWT de Fondcombe	6/9 months	Bernard BOUCHER	Marie-Christine HALLÉPÉE	US RW-GC Brockhaven SEN-

Cat	class	Owner	Breeder	Sire / Dam
	F 15/03/02			SEN of Fondcombe CHI Tavaron NOUT of Fondcombe
THAIS de Boutigny	6/9 months F 08/04/02	Annia STEPNIAK-BOUTIGNY	Annia STEPNIAK-BOUTIGNY	PTAH-HOTEP de Fondcombe RÊVE of Sweetness

Attending cats - Black Smoke

Cat	class	Owner	Breeder	Sire / Dam
CHI SENEKKW de Bélénus	CAGCI F 03/02/01	Marie-Christine HALLÉPÉE	Sandrine MAISNIER-DUFOUR	CH DANTON du Nil Blanc FAUSTINE du Nil Blanc
CH Sunrise Abycats SPEEDY	CACIB M 15/09/01	Myriam KHÉRIF	Liliane Rudel	Brockhaven SEN-SEN of Fondcombe Mas-Ree Maus OSIRIS
CH Imhotep SOBEK	CACIB M 06/09/01	Valérie DELIBES	Myriam KHÉRIF	IMHOTEP RA-LAIDACH della Dea Sekhmet PI-LAZULI Mau Sunrise Abycats
Imhotep SETHI	CAC M 06/09/01	Valérie DELIBES	Myriam KHÉRIF	IMHOTEP RA-LAIDACH della Dea Sekhmet PI-LAZULI Mau Sunrise Abycats
PR Brockhaven ANWAR of Fondcombe	CAP M Neuter 04/07/00	Marie-Christine HALLÉPÉE	Dorothea BROCKSOM	US GC Tavaron MAIMEO of Brockhaven RW-GC Brockhaven US OSIRA

Attending cats - Bronze

Cat	class	Owner	Breeder	Sire / Dam
GCHE IMHOTEP RA-LAIDACH della Dea Sekhmet	Honour M 18/03/00	Christianne SEVAL-CHAPTAL	Massimiliano ROVELLI	CHI HORUSde Joha CHI ESETvom Margelacker
CHI SENET de Fondcombe	CAGCI F 12/08/01	Marie-Christine HALLÉPÉE	Marie-Christine HALLÉPÉE	SAHOURÊ of Fondcombe Tavaron NOUT of Fondcombe
HEKET della Dea Sekhmet	CAC F 18/03/00	Joëlle CHARIER	Massimiliano ROVELLI	CHI HORUS de Joha CHI ESETvom vom Margelacker
RAHÈS-RÊ de Fondcombe	CAP M neuter 11/07/00	Paul-Henri PIOTROWSKI	Marie-Christine HALLÉPÉE	SAHOURÊ of Fondcombe Tavaron NOUT of Fondcombe
NISIS du Vieux-Pont	HC F 11/08/97	Christa ARBÈS	Henri CAYSSIAL	De Joha HATOR De Joha KISMET

Results of the special (26/10/02)

	Cat	Color	Owner	Breeder
1	Imhotep TAOURET	Silver	Myriam KHÉRIF	Myriam KHÉRIF
2	CHE Brochhaven SEN-SEN of Fondcombe	Silver	Marie-Christine HALLÉPÉE	Dorothea BROCKSOM
3	GCHE IMHOTEP RA-LAIDACH della Dea Sekhmet	Bronze	Christianne SEVAL-CHAPTAL	Massimiliano ROVELLI
4	TWT de Fondcombe	Silver	Bernard BOUCHER	Marie-Christine HALLÉPÉE
5	TEP de Fondcombe	Silver	Zoran RADOVANOVIC	Marie-Christine HALLÉPÉE
6	CHE PRINCESSE NEFERMEREN de Fondcombe	Silver	Christiane GUÉRIN	Marie-Christine HALLÉPÉE
7	CH Imhotep SOBEK	Smoke	Valérie DELIBES	Myriam KHÉRIF
8	CH SWT de Fondcombe	Silver	Christianne SEVAL-CHAPTAL	Marie-Christine HALLÉPÉE
9	THÔT de Boutigny	Silver	Michel JOB	Annia STEPNIAK-BOUTIGNY
10	GCHI IOUNYT von Skarrabäus	Silver	Myriam KHÉRIF	Sylvia HODEL-DOPLER

Best Silver: Imhotep TAOURET

Best Bronze: GCHE IMHOTEP RA-LAIDACH de la Dea Sekhmet

Best Black Smoke: CH Imhotep SOBEK

Special Mau, Aubevoye 2003

Attending cats - Silver

Cat	class	Owner	Breeder	Sire / Dam
GC, RW, GCHE Brockhaven SEN-SEN of Fondcombe	Honour M 24/03/99	Marie-Christine HALLÉPÉE	Dorothea BROCKSOM	US GC Tavaron MAUMEO of Brockhaven RW-GC Brockhaven US OSIRA
GCHI Tavaron SARINA of Fondcombe	CACE F 14/03/00	Marie-Christine HALLÉPÉE	Steve & Rebecca BERGERON	US GC Triangle ASPARET Mau of Tavaron Brockhaven JAID of Tavaron
CHI Imhotep SETHI	CAGCI M 06/09/01	Valérie DELIBES	Myriam KHÉRIF	IMHOTEP RA-LAIDACH della Dea Sekhmet PI-LAZULI Mau Sunrise Abycats
CHI SWT de Fondcombe	CAGCI F 09/06/01	Christianne SEVAL-CHAPTAL	Marie-Christine HALLÉPÉE	US RW-GC Brockhaven SEN-SEN of Fondcombe Renen de Fondcombe
CH TWT de Fondcombe	CACIB F 15/03/02	Bernard BOUCHER	Marie-Christine HALLÉPÉE	US RW-GC Brockhaven SEN-SEN of Fondcombe CHI Tavaron NOUT of Fondcombe
GC, PR Brockhaven PHARAOH of Fondcombe	CAPIB M Neuter 04/07/00	Marie-Christine HALLÉPÉE	Dorothea BROCKSOM	US GC Brockhaven MAMNOONAM DM-CH Brockhaven PHILOMENE
KHNOUMSES von Skarrabäus	CAC M 11/07/02	Myriam KHÉRIF	Silvia HODEL	CE GERONIMO von Skarrabäus IDIS CLEA von Skarrabäus
SENEKET de Fondcombe	CAC F 09/06/01	Marie-Christine HALLÉPÉE	Marie-Christine HALLÉPÉE	US RW-GC Brockhaven SEN-SEN of Fondcombe RENEN de Fondcombe
Imhotep TAOURET	CAC F 29/06/02	Myriam KHÉRIF	Myriam KHÉRIF	Sunrise Abycats SPEEDY CHI IOUNYT von Skarrabäus
TEP de Fondcombe	CAP M Neuter 07/03/02	Zoran RADOVANOVIC	Marie-Christine HALLÉPÉE	US RW-GC Brockhaven SEN-SEN of Fondcombe RESOUT de Fondcombe
TEP-NEFER de Fondcombe	3/6 month	Marie-Christine HALLÉPÉE	Marie-Christine HALLÉPÉE	CHI SENEFER de Fondcombe

Cat	class	Owner	Breeder	Sire / Dam
Manhanaria du Chaptal TARQA	3/6 months M 24/12/02	Christianne SEVAL-CHAPTAL	Christianne SEVAL-CHAPTAL	GCHI Tavaron SARINA of Fondcombe GCHE IMHOTEP RA-LAIDACH della Dea Sekhmet
TIW de Fondcombe	3/6 months M 29/12/02	Marie-Christine HALLÉPÉE	Marie-Christine HALLÉPÉE	CHI SWT de Fondcombe CHI SENEFER de Fondcombe
Manhanaria du Chaptal TANIS	3/6 months F 24/12/02	Christianne SEVAL-CHAPTAL	Christianne SEVAL-CHAPTAL	GCHI Tavaron SARINA of Fondcombe GCHE IMHOTEP RA-LAIDACH della Dea Sekhmet
Manhanaria du Chaptal THELIS	3/6 months F 29/12/02	Christianne SEVAL-CHAPTAL	Christianne SEVAL-CHAPTAL	CHI SWT de Fondcombe GCHE IMHOTEP RA-LAIDACH della Dea Sekhmet CHI SWT de Fondcombe
DIDOUFRI of Mauisha	3/6 months M 30/10/02	Pascal CARPENTIER	Isabelle DE BAKKER	De Joha AKHIM-RA of Mauisha NEHESY of Mauisha
TANGO du Wadi Sana'a	3/6 months M 25/11/02	Sylvain CHARLEUF	Guillaume & Nathalie LE BRICON	Tavaron SINOUE of BELLENUS Matiki's PHOEBE of Wadi Sana'a
Brockhaven DOT'S HEART of Fondcombe	CAP F Neuter 21/05/99	Brigitte & Nicolas ROULLEAUX	Dot's BROCKSOM	Brockhaven MAMNONAM Brockhaven PHILIMENE
CH Matiki's PHOEBE of Wadi Sana'a	CACIB F 13/07/99	Guillaume & Nathalie LE BRICON	Jan & Bonnie Wydro	OCALI SPOTS OFF THE DICE of Matiki New Kingdom NINI of Matiki

Attending cats - Black Smoke

Cat	class	Owner	Breeder	Sire / Dam
CHE SENEKKW de Bélénus	CAGCE F 03/02/01	Marie-Christine HALLÉPÉE	Sandrine MAISNIER-DUFOUR	CH DANTON du Nil Blanc FAUSTINE du Nil Blanc
CHI Imhotep SOBEK	CAGCIB M 06/09/01	Valérie DELIBES	Myriam KHÉRIF	IMHOTEP RA-LAIDACH della Dea Sekhmet PI-LAZULI Mau Sunrise Abycats
PR Brockhaven ANWAR of Fondcombe	CAPIB M Neuter 04/07/00	Marie-Christine HALLÉPÉE	Dorothea BROCKSOM	US GC Tavaron MAIMEO of Brockhaven RW-GC Brockhaven US OSIRA

Cat	class	Owner	Breeder	Sire / Dam
Imhotep TRIPHAENA CLEOPATRA	CAC F 29/06/02	Christianne SEVAL-CHAPTAL	Myriam KHÉRIF	Sunrise Abycats SPEEDY IOUNYT von Skarrabaüs

Attending cats - Bronze

Cat	class	Owner	Breeder	Sire / Dam
GCHE IMHOTEP RA-LAIDACH della Dea Sekhmet	Honour M 18/03/00	Christianne SEVAL-CHAPTAL	Massimiliano ROVELLI	CHI HORUSde Joha CHI ESETvom Margelacker
GCHI SENET de Fondcombe	CACE F 12/08/01	Marie-Christine HALLÉPÉE	Marie-Christine HALLÉPÉE	SAHOURÊ of Fondcombe Tavaron NOUT of Fondcombe
GCHI HEKET della Dea Sekhmet	CACE F 18/03/00	Joëlle CHARIER	Massimiliano ROVELLI	CHI HORUS de Joha CHI ESETvom vom Margelacker
Manhanaria du Chaptal TOUTANKHAMON	3/6 months M 29/12/02	Christianne SEVAL-CHAPTAL	Christianne SEVAL-CHAPTAL	GCHE IMHOTEP RA-LAIDACH della Dea Sekhmet CHI SWT de Fondcombe

The best on 19/04/2003)

Best variety SILVER: GCHE, GC, RW Brockhaven SEN-SEN of Fondcombe

Best variety BRONZE: GCHE IMHOTEP RA-LAIDACH de la Dea Sekhmet

Best variety SMOKE: Imhotep TRIPHAENA CLEOPATRA

BEST in SHOW male kitten 3/6 months: TANGO du Wadi Sana'a

NB: Contrary to usage, the judge chose two honor class cats for its bests.

The best on 20/04/2003)

Best adult SILVER: KHNOUMSES von Skarrabäus

Best neuter SILVER: GC, PR Brockhaven PHARAOH of Fondcombe

Best variety BRONZE: GCHI SENET de Fondcombe

Best variety SMOKE: CHI Imhotep SOBEK

Best male kitten: Manhanaria du Chaptal TARQA

Best female kitten: TIW de Fondcombe

Best Honour: GCHE, GC, RW Brockhaven SEN-SEN of Fondcombe

Results of the special (20/04/2003)

	Cat	Color	Owner	Breeder
1	GCHE, GC, RW Brockhaven SEN-SEN of Fondcombe	Silver	Marie-Christine HALLÉPÉE	Dorothea BROCKSOM
2	CHI Imhotep SOBEK	Smoke	Valérie DELIBES	Myriam KHÉRIF
3	GCHE IMHOTEP RA-LAIDACH della Dea Sekhmet	Bronze	Christianne SEVAL-CHAPTAL	Massimiliano ROVELLI
4	KHNOUMSES von Skarrabäus	Silver	Myriam KHÉRIF	Silvia HODEL
5	Manhanaria du Chaptal TARQA	Silver	Christianne SEVAL-CHAPTAL	Christianne SEVAL-CHAPTAL
6	TIW de Fondcombe	Silver	Marie-Christine HALLÉPÉE	Marie-Christine HALLÉPÉE
7	GCHI Tavaron SARINA of Fondcombe	Silver	Marie-Christine HALLÉPÉE	Steve & Rebecca BERGERON
8	GCHI SENET de Fondcombe	Bronze	Marie-Christine HALLÉPÉE	Marie-Christine HALLÉPÉE
9	GC, PR Brockhaven PHARAOH of Fondcombe	Silver Neutre	Marie-Christine HALLÉPÉE	Dorothea BROCKSOM
10	SENEKKW de Bellenus	Smoke	Marie-Christine HALLÉPÉE	Sandrine MAISNIER-DUFOUR

Best Silver: GCHE, GC, RW Brockhaven SEN-SEN of Fondcombe

Best Bronze: GCHE IMHOTEP RA-LAIDACH de la Dea Sekhmet

Best Black Smoke: CHI Imhotep SOBEK

Special, Chinagora 2003

On November 29 and 30, 2003, the Egyptian Maus organized a new meeting at Chinagora show. 21 Maus were present. This was again a great time.

Behind the scenes, the fanciers could admire the elegance of the Egyptian Mau black thanks to the presence of Ba of Fondcombe.

Attending cats - Silver

Cat	class	Owner	Breeder	Sire / Dam
GCHE Brockhaven SEN-SEN de Fondcombe	Honour M 24/03/99	Marie-Christine HALLÉPÉE	Dorothea BROCKSOM	US GC Tavaron MAUMEO of Brockhaven RW-GC Brockhaven US OSIRA
CH THELIS de Manhanaria du Chaptal	CACIB F 29/12/02	Marie-Thérèse VALLÉE	Christiane SEVAL-CHAPTAL	Imhotep della Dea Sekhmet Swt de Fondcombe
CH TWT de Fondcombe	CACIB F 15/03/02	Bernard BOUCHER	Marie-Christine HALLÉPÉE	US RW-GC Brockhaven SEN-SEN of Fondcombe CHI Tavaron NOUT of Fondcombe
GC, PR Brockhaven PHARAOH of Fondcombe	CAPIB M Neuter 04/07/00	Marie-Christine HALLÉPÉE	Dorothea BROCKSOM	US GC Brockhaven MAMNOONAM DM-CH Brockhaven PHILOMENE
DIDOUFRI of Mauïsha	CAC M 30/10/02	Pascal CARPENTIER	Isabelle DEBAKKER	De Joha AKHIM RA of Mauïsha MEHESY of Mauïsha
TEP-NEFERde Fondcombe	CAC M 24/12/02	Sandrine MAISNIER-DUFOUR	Marie-Christine HALLÉPÉE	CHI SENEFER de Fondcombe GCHI Tavaron SARINA of Fondcombe
THÔT de Boutigny	CAC M 08/04/02	Michel JOB	Annia STEPNIAK-BOUTIGNY	PTAH-HOTEP de Fondcombe RÊVE of Sweetness
TIW de Fondcombe	CAC F 24/12/02	Marie-Christine HALLÉPÉE	Marie-Christine HALLÉPÉE	CHI SENEFER de Fondcombe GCHI Tavaron SARINA of Fondcombe
TESS du Wadi Sana'a	CAC F 25/11/02	Sylvie SCHUTZ	Guillaume & Nathalie LE BRICON	Tavaron SINOUE of Belenus Matiki's PHOEBE
TANIS de Fondcombe	CAC F 07/03/02	Michel JOB	Marie-Christine HALLÉPÉE	US RW-GC Brockhaven SEN-SEN of Fondcombe RESOUT de Fondcombe

Cat	class	Owner	Breeder	Sire / Dam
SOTHIS de Fondcombe	CAC F 09/06/01	Marie-Christine HALLÉPÉE	Marie-Christine HALLÉPÉE	US RW-GC Brockhaven SEN-SEN of Fondcombe RENEN de Fondcombe
RE-SHAÏ de Fondcombe	CAP M 05/09/00	Chantal POISSON-PIOTROWSKI	Marie-Christine HALLÉPÉE	US RW-GC Brockhaven SEN-SEN of Fondcombe Fleur du Nil Blanc
SENEKET de Fondcombe	CAP F 09/06/01	Marie-Christine HALLÉPÉE	Marie-Christine HALLÉPÉE	US RW-GC Brockhaven SEN-SEN of Fondcombe RENEN de Fondcombe
TIT de Fondcombe	CAP F 07/03/02	Chantal POISSON-PIOTROWSKI	Marie-Christine HALLÉPÉE	US RW-GC Brockhaven SEN-SEN of Fondcombe RESOUT de Fondcombe
UPPITY de Fondcombe	6/10 months M 12/02/03	Aurore GIROUD	Marie-Christine HALLÉPÉE	US RW-GC Brockhaven SEN-SEN of Fondcombe GCHI SENET de Fondcombe
UDINE de Belenus	3/6 months F 16/06/03	Sandrine MAISNIER-DUFOUR	Sandrine MAISNIER-DUFOUR	Tavaron SINOUE of Belenus ORELIA de Belenus

Attending cats - Black Smoke

Chat	Classe	Propriétaire	Éleveur	Père / Mère
PRI Brockhaven ANWAR of Fondcombe	CAGPIB M Neuter 04/07/00	Marie-Christine HALLÉPÉE	Dorothea BROCKSOM	US GC Tavaron MAIMEO of Brockhaven RW-GC Brockhaven US OSIRA

Attending cats - Bronze

Cat	class	Owner	Breeder	Sire / Dam
CHI SEKHMET de Belenus	CAGCI F 11/07/00	Sandrine MAISNIER-DUFOUR	Sandrine MAISNIER-DUFOUR	Tavaron SINOUE of Belenus FAUSTINE du Nil Blanc
RAHÈS-RÊ de Fondcombe	CAP M neuter 11/07/00	Paul-Henri PIOTROWSKI	Marie-Christine HALLÉPÉE	SAHOURÊ of Fondcombe Tavaron NOUT of Fondcombe
UP-CHANGE de Fondcombe	6/10 months F 12/02/03	Marie-Christine HALLÉPÉE	Marie-Christine HALLÉPÉE	US RW-GC Brockhaven SEN-SEN of Fondcombe GCHI SENET de Fondcombe

Chat	Classe	Propriétaire	Éleveur	Père / Mère
UPSWING de Fondcombe	3/6 months M 24/07/03	Marie-Christine HALLÉPÉE	Marie-Christine HALLÉPÉE	MASLAMA of Fondcombe GCHI SENET de Fondcombe

Attending cat – Black

Cat	class	Owner	Breeder	Sire / Dam
BA de Fondcombe	HC M 24/07/03	Marie-Christine HALLÉPÉE	Marie-Christine HALLÉPÉE	MASLAMA of Fondcombe GCHI SENET de Fondcombe

Results of saturday 29/11/03

	Cat	Color	Best in variety	Best in Show
	GCHE Brochhaven SEN-SEN of Fondcombe	Silver		Best in Show Honour
	CH THELIS de Manhanaria du Chapta	Silver	Best variety	
	PR Brockhaven PHARAOH of Fondcombe	Silver		Nominated
	TIW de Fondcombe	Silver	Best variety	Nominated
	SENEKET de Fondcombe	Silver		Best in Show Femelle Neutre
	UPPITY de Fondcombe	Silver		Best in Show Chaton Mâle 6-9 mois
	UDINE de Belenus	Silver		Nominated
	PRI Brockhaven ANWAR of Fondcombe	Smoke		Nominated
	CHI SEKHMET de Belenus	Bronze		Nominated
	UPSWING de Fondcombe	Bronze	Best variety	Nominated
	UP-CHANGE de Fondcombe	Bronze		Nominated

Results of sunday 30/11/03

Cat	Color	Best in variety	Best in Show
GCHE Brochhaven SEN-SEN of Fondcombe	Silver		Best in Show Honour
CH THELIS de Manhanaria du Chapta	Silver	Best variety	Nominated
DIDOUFRI of Mauïsha	Silver		Nominated
RE-SHAI de Fondcombe	Silver		Best in Show neuter Male
UPPITY de Fondcombe	Silver	Best variety	Best in Show Male kitten 6-9 months
PRI Brockhaven ANWAR of Fondcombe	Smoke	Special prize	
CHI SEKHMET de Belenus	Bronze	Best variety	
RAHES-RE de Fondcombe	Bronze		Nominated
UPSWING de Fondcombe	Bronze	Special prize	

Special, Antony 2004

Let's note that this show was attended by 5 European Grand Champions (SEN-SEN et SENEKKW) and European Champions (SARINA, SOBEK, SENET)

Attending cats - Silver

Cat	class	Owner	Breeder	Sire / Dam
GCHE Brockhaven SEN-SEN de Fondcombe	Honour M 24/03/99	Marie-Christine HALLÉPÉE	Dorothea BROCKSOM	US GC Tavaron MAUMEO of Brockhaven RW-GC Brockhaven US OSIRA
CHE Tavaron SARINA of Fondcombe	CACE F 14/03/00	Marie-Christine HALLÉPÉE	Steve & Rebecca BERGERON	US GC Triangle ASPARET Mau of Tavaron Brockhaven JAID of Tavaron
CH THELIS de Manhanaria du Chaptal	CAGCI F 29/12/02	Marie-Thérèse VALLÉE	Christiane SEVAL-CHAPTAL	IMHOTEP RA LAIDACH della Dea Sekhmet SWT de Fondcombe
GC, PRI Brockhaven PHARAOH of Fondcombe	CAGPIB M Neuter 04/07/00	Marie-Christine HALLÉPÉE	Dorothea BROCKSOM	US GC Brockhaven MAMNOONAM DM-CH Brockhaven PHILOMENE
CH TWT de Fondcombe	CACIB F 15/03/02	Bernard BOUCHER	Marie-Christine HALLÉPÉE	US RW-GC Brockhaven SEN-SEN of Fondcombe CHI Tavaron NOUT of Fondcombe
TIW de Fondcombe	CAC F 24/12/02	Marie-Christine HALLÉPÉE	Marie-Christine HALLÉPÉE	CHI SENEFER de Fondcombe GCHI Tavaron SARINA of Fondcombe
TANGO du Wadi Sana'a	CAC M 25/11/02	Sylvain CHARLEUF	Guillaume & Nathalie LE BRICON	Tavaron SINOUE of BELLENUS Matiki's PHOEBE of Wadi Sana'a
DIDOUFRI of Mauïsha	CAC M 30/10/02	Pascal CARPENTIER	Isabelle DEBAKKER	De Joha AKHIM RA of Mauïsha NEHESY of Mauïsha
UPPITY de Fondcombe	CAC M 12/02/03	Aurore GIROUD	Marie-Christine HALLÉPÉE	US RW-GC Brockhaven SEN-SEN of Fondcombe GCHI SENET de Fondcombe
THÔT de Boutigny	CAC M 08/04/02	Christine JOB	Annia STEPNIAK-BOUTIGNY	PTAH-HOTEP de Fondcombe RÊVE of Sweetness
SOTHIS de Fondcombe	CAC F	Marie-Christine HALLÉPÉE	Marie-Christine HALLÉPÉE	US RW-GC Brockhaven SEN-

Cat	class	Owner	Breeder	Sire / Dam
	09/06/01			SEN of Fondcombe RENEN de Fondcombe
UTHER PENDRAGON de Fondcombe	6/10 month M 15/08/03	Marie-Christine HALLÉPÉE	Marie-Christine HALLÉPÉE	SEFEN de Bélénus SWNETde Fondcombe

This show is the final public event of SEN-SEN Brockhaven of Fondcombe who there and then ended his show career and his sire career after having probably been the most beautiful mau in Europe.

Attending cats - Black Smoke

Cat	class	Owner	Breeder	Sire / Dam
CHE SENEKKW de Bélénus	Honour F 03/02/01	Marie-Christine HALLÉPÉE	Sandrine MAISNIER-DUFOUR	CH DANTON du Nil Blanc FAUSTINE du Nil Blanc
CHE Imhotep SOBEK	CAGCE M 06/09/01	Valérie DELIBES	Myriam KHÉRIF	IMHOTEP RA-LAIDACH della Dea Sekhmet PI-LAZULI Mau Sunrise Abycats
PRI Brockhaven ANWAR of Fondcombe	CAGPIB M Neuter 04/07/00	Marie-Christine HALLÉPÉE	Dorothea BROCKSOM	US GC Tavaron MAIMEO of Brockhaven RW-GC Brockhaven US OSIRA

Let's note that SENEKKW is the first black smoke Egyptian Mau ever to have become European Grand Champion. SOBEK will probably be the first smoke male ever to have got this title.

Attending cats - Bronze

Cat	class	Owner	Breeder	Sire / Dam
GCHI SENET de Fondcombe	CACE F 12/08/01	Marie-Christine HALLÉPÉE	Marie-Christine HALLÉPÉE	SAHOURÊ of Fondcombe Tavaron NOUT of Fondcombe
UP-CHANGE de Fondcombe	CAC F 12/02/03	Marie-Christine HALLÉPÉE	Marie-Christine HALLÉPÉE	US RW-GC Brockhaven SEN-SEN of Fondcombe GCHI SENET de Fondcombe
UPSWING de Fondcombe	6/10 month M 24/07/03	Thérèse LEFEVRE	Marie-Christine HALLÉPÉE	MASLAMA of Fondcombe GCHI SENET de Fondcombe
UPPER EGYPT de Fondcombe	6/10 month F 24/07/03	Marie-Christine HALLÉPÉE	Marie-Christine HALLÉPÉE	MASLAMA of Fondcombe GCHI SENET de Fondcombe

Results of saturday 07/02/2004

Cat	Color	Best in variety	Best in Show
GCHE Brochhaven SEN-SEN of Fondcombe	Silver		Nominated
TIW de Fondcombe	Silver	Best variety	Nominated
PRI Brockhaven PHARAOH of Fondcombe	Silver		Nominated
TANGO du Wadi Sana'a	Silver		Best in Show Adult male
UTHER PENDRAGON de Fondcombe	Silver		Nominated
PRI Brockhaven ANWAR of Fondcombe	Smoke	Best variety	
UPSWING de Fondcombe	Bronze	Best variety	Nominated
UPPER EGYPT de Fondcombe	Bronze	3rd best female kitten	Nominated

Results of sunday 08/02/2004

Cat	Color	Best in variety	Best in Show
GCHE Brochhaven SEN-SEN of Fondcombe	Silver		Best in Show Honour
TANGO du Wadi Sana'a	Silver		Best in Show Adult male
CH TWT de Fondcombe	Silver		Best in Show Adult female
PRI Brockhaven PHARAOH of Fondcombe	Silver		Best in Show Neuter male
UTHER PENDRAGON de Fondcombe	Silver	Best variety	Best in Show Male 6/9 months **Best of Best**
UPSWING de Fondcombe	Bronze	3rd best male kitten	
UPPER EGYPT de Fondcombe	Bronze	Best variety	Best in Show Female 6/9 months

CHE Imhotep SOBEK	Smoke	Best variety	

Special, Sannois 2006

Attending cats - Silver

Cat	class	Owner	Breeder	Sire / Dam
ANTYOU du Dieu Thot	CAC F 02/01/05	Christine JOB	Christine JOB	THOT de Boutigny VERY BASTET de Bélénus
DIDOUFRI of Mauïsha	CAP M Neuter 30/10/02	Pascal CARPENTIER	Isabelle DEBAKKER	De Joha AKHIM RA of Mauïsha NEHESY of Mauïsha
GCI TWT de Fondcombe	CACE F 15/03/02	Bernard BOUCHER	Marie-Christine HALLÉPÉE	US RW-GC Brockhaven SEN-SEN of Fondcombe CHI Tavaron NOUT of Fondcombe
CH V. ENAK de la Manhanaria du Chaptal	CACIB M 27/02/04	Christiane SEVAL-CHAPTAL	Christiane SEVAL-CHAPTAL	IMHOTEP RA LAIDACH della Dea Sekhmet SWT de Fondcombe
Schooiertjes ZORA	6/10 months M 01/06/05	Serge & Valérie BORCARD	Hans & Olga GARRETSEN	DW Matiki's AMULET Schooiertjes ANNY
CH UTHER PENDRAGON de Fondcombe	CACIB * M 15/08/03	Marie-Christine HALLÉPÉE	Marie-Christine HALLÉPÉE	SEFEN de Bélénus SWNETde Fondcombe
CH VELLEDA de Fondcombe	CACIB * F 18/06/04	Marie-Christine HALLÉPÉE	Marie-Christine HALLÉPÉE	MASLAMA of Fondcombe Tavaron SARINA of Fondcombe
Maullenium MESKHEMET of Fondcombe	CAC F 22/02/05	Marie-Christine HALLÉPÉE	Dorothy MARDULIER	Brockhaven SUNAMI of Maullenium Maullenium CALYPSO
VANAOS de l'Arbre Perché	CAP M Neuter 17/07/04	Christelle CAILLEUX-SABATIER	Christelle CAILLEUX-SABATIER	DANTON du Nil Blanc TY'BONBON du Wadi Sana'a
Shaimau MIKALOU of l'Arbre Perché	6/10 months M 26/05/05	Christelle CAILLEUX-SABATIER	Eric TURCOTTE	Nile Blue MIHOS of Shaimau Mavisha DISHASHA

Attending cats - Black Smoke

Cat	class	Owner	Breeder	Sire / Dam
CHI VICTOIRE DE KADESH du Fort de la Bosse Marnière	CAGCI F 06/06/04	Bernard BOUCHER	Bernard BOUCHER	DANTON du Nil Blanc TWT de Fondcombe

Cat	class	Owner	Breeder	Sire / Dam
Pr Imhotep TRIPHAENA CLEOPATRA	CAPIB F Neuter 29/06/02	Christiane SEVAL-CHAPTAL	Myriam KHERIF	Sunrise Abycats SPEEDY IOUNYT von Skarrabaus
NUAGE DANSANT de Mu Arde	6/10 mois M Neuter 11/02/05	Serge & Valérie BORCARD	Serge & Valérie BORCARD	JAMIN el Men Nefer LILITH von Sopte en Re

Attending cats - Bronze

Cat	class	Owner	Breeder	Sire / Dam
V-GEB de l'Arbre Perché	CAP M Neuter 13/07/04	Christine JOB	Christelle CAILLEUX-SABATIER	DANTON du Nil Blanc TY'BONBON du Wadi Sana'a
GCHE IMHOTEP RA-LAIDACH della Dea Sekhmet	Honour M 18/03/00	Christianne SEVAL-CHAPTAL	Massimiliano ROVELLI	CHI HORUSde Joha CHI ESETvom Margelacker
NIKITA de Mu Aral	6/10 months F Neuter 11/02/05	Serge & Valérie BORCARD	Serge & Valérie BORCARD	JAMIN el Men Nefer LILITH von Sopte en Re
VANARAH de l'Arbre Perché	CAC M 17/07/04	Christelle CAILLEUX-SABATIER	Christelle CAILLEUX-SABATIER	DANTON du Nil Blanc TY'BONBON du Wadi Sana'a

Results of saturday 11/02/2006

Best variety
Nominated to best in show short hair 6/10 months female
Maullenium MESKHEMET of Fondcombe

Results of sunday 12/02/2006

Best variety
Best Egyptian Mau
Nominated to best in show short hair 6/10 months female
Nominated to supreme best
Maullenium MESKHEMET of Fondcombe

Best in show short hair neuter male
V-GEB de l'arbre perché

Rankings of the special		
Cat	Color	Rankings
Maullenium MESHKEMET of Fondcombe	Silver	1 st
V. ENAK de la Manhanaria du Chaptal	Silver	2 nd
V-GEB de l'arbre perché	Bronze	3 rd
VANAOS de l'Arbre Perché	Silver	4 th
Schooiertjes ZORA	Silver	5 th

Special, Poissy 2007

For the first time in Europe, over 30 Maus together in a single show!

Attending cats - Silver

Cat	class	Owner	Breeder	Sire / Dam
AKTHY de Fondcombe	CAC M 29/11/05	Sandrine MAISNIER-DUFOUR	Marie-Christine HALLÉPÉE	MASLAMA de Fondcombe TIW de Fondcombe
ANTYOU du Dieu Thot	CAC F 02/01/05	Christine JOB	Christine JOB	THOT de Boutigny VERY BASTET de Bélénus
ATOUM du Dieu Thôt	CAP M 00/00/05	Stéphane JAFFRAY	Christine JOB	THOT de Boutigny VERY BASTET de Bélénus
CH BABY ICE de l'Arbre Perché	CACIB F 17/05/05	Christelle CAILLEUX-SABATIER	Christelle CAILLEUX-SABATIER	Shaimau MITAKAU of l'Arbre Perché VAHAVRIE de l'Arbre Perché
BATYT de Fondcombe	CAC F 20/11/06	Bernard BOUCHER	Marie-Christine HALLÉPÉE	UTHER PENDRAGON de Fondcombee Maullenium MESHKEMET of Fondcombe
BEAUTIFUL RAMSES du Dieu Thôt	HC M 30/05/06	Anne BLANCHARD	Christine JOB	THOT de Boutigny VERY BASTET de Bélénus
BISOU de Fondcombe	CAC F 20/11/06	Sandrine MAISNIER-DUFOUR	Marie-Christine HALLÉPÉE	UTHER PENDRAGON de Fondcombee Maullenium MESHKEMET of Fondcombe
BIAYT de Fondcombe	CAC F 13/10/06	Sandrine MAISNIER-DUFOUR	Marie-Christine HALLÉPÉE	UTHER PENDRAGON de Fondcombee VELLEDA de Fondcombe
BOUBASTIS du Dieu Thôt	CAC F 07/09/06	Christine JOB	Christine JOB	UPITY de Fondcombe ANTYOU du Dieu Thôt
BOUKHIS de la Manaharia du Chaptal	CAP M 07/04/06	Bernadette LEROUX	Christiane SEVAL-CHAPTAL	IMOTHEP RA LAIDACH della Dea Sekhmet SWT de Fondcombe
BNT-WRT de Bélénus	CAC F 17/08/06	Sandrine MAISNIER-DUFOUR	Sandrine MAISNIER-DUFOUR	TEP NEFER de Fondcombe UDINE de Bélénus
CALIS de l'Arbre Perché	3/6 months M 27/05/07	Christelle CAILLEUX-SABATIER	Christelle CAILLEUX-SABATIER	Shaimau MIKALOU of l'Arbre Perché VAHOURI de l'Arbre Perché

Cat	class	Owner	Breeder	Sire / Dam
CALLIMAQUE du Dieu Thôt	HC F 02/05/07	Christine JOB	Christine JOB	THOT de Boutigny VERY BASTET de Bélénus
CHEDI de Fondcombe	3/6 months F 12/03/07	Marie-Christine HALLÉPÉE	Marie-Christine HALLÉPÉE	Maullenium AMUN-RÂ de Fondcombe VELLEDA de Fondcombe
CHEYK MAHAT de la Manhanaria du Chapatal	3/6 months M 29/05/07	Christiane SEVAL-CHAPTAL	Christiane SEVAL-CHAPTAL	IMOTHEP RA LAIDACH della Dea Sekhmet SWT de Fondcombe
CHOU du Dieu Thôt	HC M 02/05/07	Christine JOB	Christine JOB	THOT de Boutigny VERY BASTET de Bélénus
CORUS de l'Arbre Perché	3/6 months M 27/05/07	Christelle CAILLEUX-SABATIER	Christelle CAILLEUX-SABATIER	Shaimau MIKALOU of l'Arbre Perché VAHOURI de l'Arbre Perché
CORISIS de l'Arbre Perché	3/6 mois M 27/05/07	Christelle CAILLEUX-SABATIER	Christelle CAILLEUX-SABATIER	Shaimau MIKALOU of l'Arbre Perché VAHOURI de l'Arbre Perché
GCI Maulenium AMUN-RA of Fondcombe	CACE M 20/09/05	Marie-Christine HALLÉPÉE	Dorothy MARDULIER	Brockhaven TSUNAMI of Maullenium Maullenium's RAZMAUTA/Z
GCI Maulenium MESHKEMET of Fondcombe	CACE F 22/02/05	Marie-Christine HALLÉPÉE	Dorothy MARDULIER	Brockhaven TSUNAMI of Maullenium Maullenium CALYPSO
OUABOU de Mu Area	CAC M 15/08/06	Christine JOB	Serge et Valérie BROCARD	NUAGE DANSANT de Mu Area Schooieryjes ZORA
TANIS de Fondcombe	CAC F 07/03/02	Christine JOB	Marie-Christine HALLÉPÉE	Brockhaven SEN-SEN of Fondcombe RESOUT de Fondcombe
CH TEP-NEFER de Fondcombe	CACIB M 24/12/02	Sandrine MAISNIER-DUFOUR	Marie-Christine HALLÉPÉE	SENEFER de Fondcombe Tavaron SARINA of Fondcombe
CI THÔT de Boutigny	CAGCI M 08/04/02	Christine JOB	Annia STEPNIAK-BOUTIGNY	PTAH-HOTEP de Fondcombe RÊVE of Sweetness
CE TWT de Fondcombe	CAGCE F 15/03/02	Bernard BOUCHER	Marie-Christine HALLÉPÉE	US RW-GC Brockhaven SEN-SEN of Fondcombe CHI Tavaron NOUT of Fondcombe
CE UTHER PENDRAGON de Fondcombe	CAGCE M 15/08/03	Marie-Christine HALLÉPÉE	Marie-Christine HALLÉPÉE	SEFEN de Bélénus SWNET de Fondcombe
GCI V. ENAK de la Manhanaria du Chaptal	CACE M 27/02/04	Christiane SEVAL-CHAPTAL	Christiane SEVAL-CHAPTAL	IMHOTEP RA LAIDACH della Dea Sekhmet SWT de Fondcombe

Attending cats - Black Smoke

Cat	class	Owner	Breeder	Sire / Dam
CH BLUE VELVET de Ramesseum	CACIB F 07/05/06	Christiane SEVAL-CHAPTAL	Nathalie VIDAL-TERRIER	V. ENAK de la Manhanaria du Chaptal V. MENEFER de Ramesseum
CH BERGAMOTTE de Ramesseum	CACIB F 07/05/06	Christelle CAILLEUX-SABATIER	Nathalie VIDAL-TERRIER	V. ENAK de la Manhanaria du Chaptal V. MENEFER de Ramesseum
GCI NUAGE DANSANT de Mu Arae	CACE M 11/02/05	Serge & Valérie BORCARD	Serge & Valérie BORCARD	JAMIN el Men Nefer LILITH von Sopte en Re
CI VERY BASTET de Bélénus	CAGCI F 24/01/04	Christine JOB	Sandrine MAISNIER-DUFOUR	TEP NEFER de Fondcombe SEKHMET de Bélénus

Attending cats - Bronze

Cat	class	Owner	Breeder	Sire / Dam
BAKKIS du Dieu Thôt	CAP M Neuter 07/09/06	Christine JOB	Christine JOB	UPITY de Fondcombe ANTYOU du Dieu Thôt
CHEOPS de l'Arbre Perché	6/10 months M 04/04/07	Patricia DESLOGES	Christelle CAILLEUX-SABATIER	VANARAH de l'Arbre Perché Shaimau AMALIS de l'Arbre Perché
CHEOPSETH CHIARA de l'Arbre Perché	6/10 months F 04/04/07	Mme MONZELIN	Christelle CAILLEUX-SABATIER	VANARAH de l'Arbre Perché Shaimau AMALIS de l'Arbre Perché
CHEOPSIS CHIARA de l'Arbre Perché	6/10 months F 04/04/07	Patricia DESLOGES	Christelle CAILLEUX-SABATIER	VANARAH de l'Arbre Perché Shaimau AMALIS de l'Arbre Perché
CHRONOS de l'Arbre Perché	6/10 months M 04/04/07	Janick DELEDICQ	Christelle CAILLEUX-SABATIER	VANARAH de l'Arbre Perché Shaimau AMALIS de l'Arbre Perché
CLEOPATRE de la Manaharia du Chaptal	3/6 months F 29/05/07	Christiane SEVAL-CHAPTAL	Christiane SEVAL-CHAPTAL	IMHOTEP RA LAIDACH della Dea Sekhmet SWT de Fondcombe
GPI V-GEB de l'Arbre Perché	CAPE M Neuter	Christine JOB	Christelle CAILLEUX-SABATIER	DANTON du NIL Blanc TY'BONBON du Wadi San'a

Results of Sunday 07/10/2007

Best variety
Best Egyptian Mau
Best kitten
Supreme Best of the show
CHEOPSETH CHIARA de l'Arbre Perché

Rankings of the special		
Cat	Color	Rankings
CHEOPSETH CHIARA de l'Arbre Perché	Bronze	1 st
BLUE VELVET de Ramesseum	Smoke	2 nd
CORISIS de l'Arbre Perché	Silver	3 rd
BERGAMOTTE de Ramesseum	Smoke	4 th
CORUS de l'Arbre Perché	Silver	5 th
BABY ICE de l'Arbre Perché	Silver	6 th
CHEYK MAHAT de la Manhanaria du Chapatal	Silver	7 th
BIAYT de Fondcombe	Silver	8 th
CHRONOS de l'Arbre Perché	Bronze	9 th
CHEDI de Fondcombe	Silver	10 th

Yep, for the first time the spectacular look of silver cats did not stop the bronze and smoke cats to rise for first!

Special, Monaco 2011

Under the patronage of SAS Albert de Monaco.

Attending cats – Silver

Cat	class	Owner	Breeder	Sire / Dam
CH ELIORA du Fort de la Bosse Marnière	CAGCIB F 11/04/09	Patrick LE COUSTUMER	Bernard BOUCHER	CH AKHTY de Fondcombe GCI VICTOIRE DE QADESH du Fort de la Bose Marnière
GCE TWT de Fondcombe	Honneur F 15/03/02	Bernard BOUCHER	Marie-Christine HALLÉPÉE	US RW-GC Brockhaven SEN-SEN of Fondcombe CHI Tavaron NOUT of Fondcombe
FISET du Fort de la Bosse Marnière	3/6 months F 12/08/10	Bernard BOUCHER	Bernard BOUCHER	BAA-LAT du Fort de la Bosse Marnière CE BATYT de Fondcombe
CE BATYT de Fondcombe	GCE F 20/11/06	Bernard BOUCHER	Marie-Christine HALLÉPÉE	UTHER PENDRAGON de Fondcombee Maullenium MESHKEMET of Fondcombe
FYLGJA du Fort de la Bosse Marnière	3/6 months F 12/08/10	Séverine MANUEL	Bernard BOUCHER	BAA-LAT du Fort de la Bosse Marnière CE BATYT de Fondcombe
FEARWEN du Fort de la Bosse Marnière	6/10 months F 03/04/10	Marc KONRAD	Bernard BOUCHER	CE DJOSER de Minas Tirith CE VICTOIRE DE QADESH du Fort de la Bose Marnière
FAROS du Fort de la Bosse Marnière	6/10 months M 03/04/10	Marc KONRAD	Bernard BOUCHER	CE DJOSER de Minas Tirith CE VICTOIRE DE QADESH du Fort de la Bose Marnière
CE Djoser de Minas Tirith	GCE M 17/02/08	Bernard BOUCHER	Sylvie SCHUTZ	BECH SETHIS de Minas Tirith AMARIË de Minas Tirith
CI SALIME von Skarrabeus	CAGCIB F 25/06/09	Catherine OSTERMANN	Sylvia HODEL	CH RE SAHDI von Scarrabeaus CH O SIRI von Skarrabeaus

Attending cats - Black Smoke

Cat	class	Owner	Breeder	Sire / Dam
CE VICTOIRE DE QADESH du Fort de la Bosse Marnière	GCE F 06/06/04	Bernard BOUCHER	Bernard BOUCHER	CH DANTON du Nil Blanc GCE TWT de Fondcombe
CI BLUE VELVET de Ramesseum	CAGCIB F 07/05/06	Christiane SEVAL-CHAPTAL	Nathalie VIDAL-TERRIER	V. ENAK de la Manhanaria du Chaptal V. MENEFER de Ramesseum
Manaharia du Chaptal FELINE	3/6 months F 31/08/10	Christiane SEVAL-CHAPTAL	Christiane SEVAL-CHAPTAL	GCE IMHOTEP RA-LAIDACH Della Dea Sekmet CI BLUE VELVET de Ramesseum

Attending cats - Bronze

Cat	class	Owner	Breeder	Sire / Dam
Maunarch FLORINA of Amiel Goshen	CAC F 13/03/10	Patrick LE COUSTUMER	Daniel PIERCE	GC Ramah Mau TAN MAN CH Sharbees PAPYUS Maukarama
Manaharia du Chaptal FAREK	3/6 months F 31/08/10	Christiane SEVAL-CHAPTAL	Christiane SEVAL-CHAPTAL	GCE IMHOTEP RA-LAIDACH Della Dea Sekmet CI BLUE VELVET de Ramesseum

Attending cats - Black

Cat	class	Owner	Breeder	Sire / Dam
Manaharia du Chaptal FARAON	3/6 months F 31/08/10	Christiane SEVAL-CHAPTAL	Christiane SEVAL-CHAPTAL	GCE IMHOTEP RA-LAIDACH Della Dea Sekmet CI BLUE VELVET de Ramesseum

Results of sunday 30/01/2011

Rewars were distributed by SAR Caroline de Hanovre.

Rankings of the special		
Cat	Color	Rankings
CH ELIORA du Fort de la Bosse Marnière	Silver	1 st
GCE TWT de Fondcombe	Silver	2 nd
Maunarch FLORINA of Amiel Goshen	Bronze	3 rd
FISET du Fort de la Bosse Marnière	Silver	4 th
CE BATYT de Fondcombe	Silver	5 th
CE VICTOIRE DE QADESH du Fort de la Bosse Marnière	Smoke	6 th
FYLGJA du Fort de la Bosse Marnière	Silver	7 th
FEARWEN du Fort de la Bosse Marnière	Silver	8 th
FAROS du Fort de la Bosse Marnière	Silver	9 th
CI BLUE VELVET de Ramesseum	Smoke	10 th

EUROPEAN CHAMPIONS AND GRAND CHAMPIONS

In Europe, several organizations are issuing titles. Points earned at shows and titles gotten are in principle recognized from one organization to another. This has not always been true.
In particular, the supreme title is European Grand Champion, but the FIFe issues European Champion as its highest title. Both of these supreme titles are of equivalent difficulty...

CE VASAR

Breeder: Mme PERNIOLA - chatterie de Joha

Owner: Dianick MASSON - chatterie du Nil Blanc

CE ELENDRIL du Nil Blanc

Breeder: Dianick MASSON - chatterie du Nil Blanc

Owner: Didier HALLÉPÉE - Chatterie de Fondcombe

Best Egyptian Mau of FIFe World championship in Milan (I)

GCE IMHOTEP RA-LAIDACH della Dea Sekhmet

Breeder: Barbara ROVELLI - chatterie della Dea Sekhmet
Owner: Christiane SEVAL-CHAPTAL

GCE, GC, RW Brockhaven SEN-SEN of Fondcombe

Breeder: Dorothea BROCKSOM - Brockhaven cattery

Owner: Didier HALLÉPÉE - Chatterie de Fondcombe

GCE Princesse NEFERMEREN de Fondcombe

Photo Christophe Hermeline/Doxicat

Breeder: Marie-Christine HALLÉPÉE - Chatterie de Fondcombe

Owner: Christiane GUÉRIN - Chatterie des Horizons de Bastet

GCE SENEKKW de Bélénus

Breeder: Sandrine MAISNIER-DUFOUR – Chatterie de Bélénus

Owner: Didier HALLÉPÉE - Chatterie de Fondcombe

GCE, CH (CFA) Tavaron's SARINA of Fondcombe

Breeder: Steve & Becki BERGERON - Tavaron cattery

Owner: Didier HALLÉPÉE - Chatterie de Fondcombe

CE SENET de Fondcombe

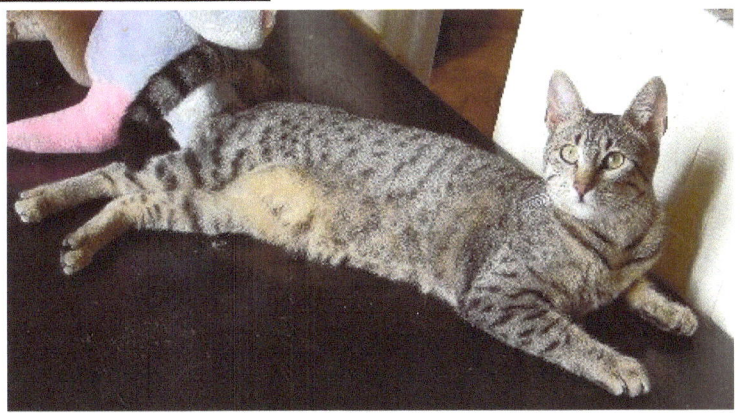

Breeder: Didier HALLÉPÉE - Chatterie de Fondcombe

Owner: Didier HALLÉPÉE - Chatterie de Fondcombe

CE Imhotep SOBEK

Breeder: Myriam KHERIF - Chatterie d'Imhotep

Owner: Valérie DELIBES

THE MAU AT HOME

A breed cat is a cat which meets a recognized standard thanks to its filiation, this being certified by a document called a pedigree.

For a cat to belong to a breed permits you to hope strongly that it will have the essential characteristics of this breed, both in terms of beauty and of character.

A cat, whether a breed one or a domestic one, is a companion which will occupy an important place in your life. Nobody doubts that it will be pleasant to live with and will enjoy a good health.
But, how to choose our future companion?

<u>Choosing a kitten</u>
In any case, after having had information by phone, you must go to the spot and ask to visit the refuge or the breeding place. It's the only way that you will be able to verify the conditions of life and hygiene of your kitten. If your visit is not permitted or is only partial, then it is better if you go elsewhere (there may be some valid reasons why something must be kept hidden from you).

Before choosing, examine the cat: its hair must be nice (a dull hair is often a symptom of bad health) and it must not be apathetic. Pass your hand against the grain of the hair in order to be sure that there are no problems (mycosis, fleas, etc.). Ask if it has undergone an anthelmintic treatment and when the same will have to be done again. Do not forget to have a look at the ears (by means of a cotton swab, helped by the breeder), to verify that there is no mange. These simple controls will avoid you several disappointments: some cats, gathered together and in bad health, may in the end prove much more expensive than a breed cat.

Ensure also that it has been socialized: if it has not been sufficiently manipulated since its youngest age, it risks being savage. But / you must not confound savage with timid: when taken by the nape, a timid cat will relax its muscles, whilst an unsocial cat will contract them and curve its body: probably, it will be very difficult to / make it sociable.
Finally, choose it following your taste, for its beauty, its character or after any other criteria of your choice.

Formalities
Do not forget that a kitten is not to be separated from its mother until it is three months old, otherwise its education will never be complete.

Ensure also that the kitten has been vaccinated (typhus and acute rhinitis). Usually, the first vaccination is effected when it is two months old. The second one, a month later. It is not possible to do the second earlier, as the immunity system of the cat is not yet complete before three months of age. You can however purchase your kitten before the second vaccination, provided you will vaccinate it when the right time comes. If you are travelling abroad, it can be compulsory to vaccinate it against rabies; this is also a good precaution as your cat may come into contact with unknown cats, for instance during an show.

The cat may be identified by means of a chip, which in some countries is compulsory. And it is also compulsory for crossing boundaries.

The indispensable documents your cat must have are: health book, contract of purchase or of transfer and pedigree if it is a breed cat. If you buy a cat abroad, its European passport will allow you to take it home with you.

Now, you have just to transport your companion (have you thought of the right type of kennel for this?).

If the breeder has not yet done this, have it undergo a test for the FIV FeLV (Feline leukaemia virus, "cats AIDS" – not transmissible to humans) and, in any case, have it inoculated against the FeLV (the vaccine against the FIV does not exist). Do not forget to treat it regularly against worms. Should you have any doubts about its health status, have it visited by your vet before it comes into contact with the other animals you have.

In any case, you have to know, if it goes out regularly, that there is a risk one day of its not coming back: it can get lost, be adopted, stolen, run over by a car. It can even make some bad meetings – close to our house, downtown, a cat has been wounded by a beech-marten. It can also meet other felines, fight with them, contract the PIF, the FIV or the FeLV (which is, as they say, the first cause of demise for felines), or contaminate the other cats at home. We have to keep in mind that the average lifetime of a feral cat is 2 or 3 years whereas an apartment cat can live 15 or even 20 years.

Therefore, if you love it, if you care for it, keep it in security, at home. If you can, re-arrange a part of the garden for it (fenced in and covered / with a net – some recommend an electrified fence). If you do not have a garden, and your cat tends to go out, you can place a net or a mosquito-net across the windows. You can also fence in a balcony if you live in an apartment (and if the co-ownership rules allow it).

Do not forget that, if it has been operated on, it will be less attracted by the outside world and will prefer the warmth of its cosy home.

Arriving at home

As soon as it has arrived, you have to show it round the house. Immediately, let it see the litter and the spot for its food. Then let it walk around wherever it will be allowed to go, so it will begin to see its new territory. Do not forget to introduce it to its new friends, if any (but never place them face to face!). Let them grumble, smell, but never force the contact on them if they prefer to avoid it: some may be jealous and will then need some time getting used to the new- comer

If it's a rather aged cat and a little timid, let it choose its own shelter (under the bed?) and place the food and the litter close to it: it will come out when it feels it has found a lasting and loving home (this may require months for a cat having experienced several abandonments – do not lose your temper!).

And then as early as the first evening, give it some... bad habits, placing it near you on the bed....

Later, the only thing to do will be to cuddle it regularly. The more loved it will be, the more loving it will be.

If there are already other animals at home, a wise thing may be to keep the new-comer with you for a few days in your room, separated from the other animals. In this way, it will have time to get used to you and to its new habitat and will be prepared for the others' presence, which, in any case, it will have already smelled out. The first contact will be easier for everybody.

May the cat go out?

If a cat has not been accustomed to getting out, it will not miss external life. The cat becomes attached to the place it lives in, more so than to the need/ for space. On the contrary, if the cat has always lived on the roads, it will be a difficult thing to get it used to staying indoors.

The cat is an inquisitive animal. It loves to know what's happening on the other side of the door. As soon as it has become acquainted with its new territory, it loves to widen it by exploring new horizons. But it also likes a limited space and it satisfies its need for security. Everyone has a right to have his or her own contradictions...

A cat can live very happily in an apartment. But if it gets used to going out, it will not stand the confinement any more. At the beginning, it will keep close to the house (unless it does not get lost on its first going out...), but, gradually, it will widen its territory and will even go very far away. The cold does not disturb it, whilst humidity and the rain can be dangerous for the least resistant specimens.

Some health suggestions

The following are just some basic and incomplete suggestions. But, maybe, you will find in them some valuable ideas. Do not hesitate to get information from your vet, the breeder who sold you the cat or from the friends who have had cats for some time.

Grooming

Grooming is not compulsory for a shorthair cat. It is in any case useful for the beauty and the health of your cat. It is also a special moment between you two (even if some cats are reluctant to be groomed at the beginning, they are grateful for any care which cannot be done by them).

You can do the grooming by yourself or ask for help in holding the cat. A little firmness will be sufficient to hold it motionless, but without exaggerating. Depending on its character, it will be fully co-operative or somewhat savage...

Eyes

Clean them with a wet compress in order to wipe off the small secretions. If the cat's eyes are running a little, put some drops of physiological serum in each eye. If the eyes are often runningand if the third eyelid is visible, then see the veterinary surgeon.

Ears

They are to be cleaned with a cotton swab imbibed with warm water. In this way you can take off the earwax. If the cotton comes out with dark brown or black traces, it can be some mange – nothing serious, but consult the vet. Of course, do not push the swabs into the inner ear.

Claws

Never take them off a cat's paw, it is an invalidating practice, and even forbidden. But you can trim its nails. To do so, hold a paw firmly, incline it to get the nails out one at a time and cut the tip off with a nail-clipper without touching the pink part. You can be content with the front paws. In this way, it will cause less hurt to itself while scratching any part of its body. And on the other hand this is compulsory before attending an show.

Hair

First thing, it's a matter of taking off the dead hair. The cat can do this by itself, but the hair, then, will obstruct the alimentary tract and cause it to vomit on your best carpet (not on the others, of course). Taking care of the fur is particularly useful when moulting time comes. A cat with semi-long hair should be cleaned at least once or twice a week. A shorthair cat, at least once or twice a month. For short hair, utilize a card or a brush with rubber prongs. Brush the coat up and down or against the nap to get the mantle smooth. For the medium long hair, utilize a comb with rather long prongs (there are particularly suitable combs with rotating prongs) to disentangle the fur and take off the dead hair. Do not forget the belly. Finally, blow hard on the collarette and the tail.

Bath

More or less appreciated, depending on the cat. Indispensable when it is too dirty, or if it has been suffering from diarrhoea and is very dirty after that, or when you wish to make it particularly nice (Turkish Angoras before a show). Use lukewarm water and a gentle shampoo holding the cat firmly (have you trimmed the claws beforehand?). Rinse abundantly in order to take off any trace of the shampoo. Dry it well wrapping it in a towel and rubbing it. Then complete the drying up with the hair-dryer (carefully, as cats do not like its noise very much, and do not hold it too close, otherwise it's too hot). Then let it go, it will start cleaning itself immediately...

Litter

It needs a small basin for its litter. A small box with a cover and door will partly avoid the bad odours, but some cats will require you to take off the door. You have to reckon one basin for every two or three cats.

As far as the contents are concerned, there are several kinds of products. Do not hesitate about choosing the best quality, it will be better. Clay sands agglomerate the droppings well and it will be sufficient for you to take off the pellets which will form. Some not too good sands stick to the paws. Granulates transform the urine into powder. Then, this sand is to be taken off. There are silicate litters shaped like small transparent crystals: in addition to being of similar quality and using sands, they have the advantage to be very light. In any case, empty the litter occasionally to clean up the basin and change the product. Make the litter morning and evening, this will be appreciated by your cat.

If you have a huge number of cats, place a sufficient number of litters around. And do not hesitate to control them several times a day, as several of them may be utilizing the same facility.

The cat is a very clean animal. If it does not like the litter, or if it is dirty, it will go elsewhere...

Some of them are attracted by sink. It cannot be helped.

If it pees everywhere?
There is a reason for that, usually. It can be its way of protesting if the litter is dirty. It can act also in this way as a signal for a diarrhoea or other health problems.

It may be a behaviour problem (too many cats, a too ample territory, badly chosen litter location). A first solution is to place the litter where it pees (later on, it can be moved to another place). If this is not sufficient, you can try to reduce the territory: not too large a room, where it will have its bed, litter and food (and its cuddles). When it is clean again, the territory may be widened progressively.

If it's an adult male, to spray its urine is a normal behaviour. In order to avoid this inconvenience, the males not meant for reproduction can be castrated. It is much more pleasant for them and for you.

Castration can be effected without any drawbacks starting from the third month of age. This has no consequences on the development of the cat.

Food
Wet food and dry food (croquettes) are available. Nowadays croquettes are adapted to the health of the cat. Foodstuffs for cats contain taurine, which is indispensable for them (and cause itches to dogs).

Dry food has the advantage of producing fewer faeces...

The food found in stock farms or at the vet's are more balanced and poor in appetisers: the cat will eat only what is necessary and will remain more slender.

Your cat may appreciate the food of supermarkets, but, be careful, if it is a delicate cat, it will have diarrhoeas. In such case, change to farm or vet food.

The cat doesn't like changes of food; proceed progressively. It is not interested in varying tastes: this is a pleasure mainly for its master.

In any case, if it is greedy, it will come and steal the food in your dish.

Do not give milk: once grownup, it does not digest it well. As concerns kittens not yet weaned, give them special milk only.

Affection

Most important, it is badly in need of love. The more you will give, the more you will get.

On the very first evening, welcome it on your bed. Once there, it will be at your height and will not feel towered over anymore. And that is the special time for cuddles.

Love it as it is (greedy? petty thief? quiet or lively, looking for fondness or calm, depending on the hours, at times even an insolent scoundrel). Please, know that a cat cannot be trained, but can be educated (in any case it will not fail to make some mischief, but it will be aware of what it is doing and will stop the moment you intervene).

Talk to it. It feels your affection and, at times, will reply to you.

If it does too many wrong things when you are not present, that is because it's getting bored. Maybe it's in need of a small companion. If you have two kittens, they will spend their time playing instead of doing wrong things.

And if it is really impossible, are you sure that you are really a suitable master for a cat?

Diarrhoeas

When a cat is suffering from them, it frequently evacuates outside the litter. And it is its way of showing it's sick.

This is often due to an unsuitable food diet. Ask the veterinary surgeon or a friend breeder for advice. The croquettes found at their places are often the right answer.

The problem may be caused by the lack of vermicide action: check its health book.

Fevers, colds, etc

If your cat is sick, consult the vet.

The first warning symptom lies in a change of behaviour, it is less reactive, remains in its corner instead of coming up to you for cuddles, and it is too quiet.

If it is feverish, the truffle and the ears are warmer. You can check its temperature by means of a clinical thermometer.

If an antibiotic treatment is prescribed, do not forget that it must last at least five days to be fully effective.

QUOTATIONS ABOUT CATS

Inscription on the Royal Tombs at Thebes

Thou art the Great Cat, the avenger of the Gods, and the judge of words, and the president of the sovereign chiefs and the governor of the holy Circle; thou art indeed...the Great Cat.

Anonymous quotations

A cat can climb down from a tree without the assistance of the fire department or any other agency. The proof is, no one has ever seen a cat's skeleton in a tree.
Unknown

A cat has two left feet. However, there is no one so skilful!
Unknown

A cat is an example of sophistication minus civilization.
Unknown

A cat sees us as dogs... A cat sees himself as a human.
Unknown

A cat sleeps fat, yet walks thin.
Unknown

A cat will assume the shape of its container.
Unknown

A nice woman he has the man who loves cats.
Unknown

A thing of beauty, strength, and grace lies behind that whiskered face.
Unknown

Always look around when your cat gazes behind you with that intent look in her eyes. Some day there might actually be something there.
Unknown

An immobile cat still has open eyes.
Unknown

And if such a story has a moral, it surely must be that it is dangerous indeed to jump at conclusions.
Unknown

As he loves his cat, so he loves his wife.
Unknown

Cats have not been put on a pedestal, they get on to it themselves
Unknown

Cats are trying to teach us that in nature, not everything is required to have a role to play.
Unknown

Cats are experiments in consciousness with limited intelligence, humans are experiments in intelligence with limited consciousness.
Unknown

Cats understand our feelings. They don't care about them, but they understand them
Unknown

Civilization is defined by the presence of cats.
Unknown

Dogs bark, cats mew, but what do ants do?
Unknown

Every dog has his day – but nights belong to cats.
Unknown

Every life should have nine cats.
Unknown

With cats, the future belongs to those who lick themselves early.
Unknown

French novelist Colette was a firm cat-lover. When she was in the U.S. she saw a cat sitting in the street. She went over to talk to it and the two of them mewed at each other for a friendly minute. Colette turned to her companion and exclaimed, Enfin ! Someone who speaks French.
Unknown

God made the cat in order to give man the pleasure of caressing the tiger.
Unknown (ascribed to Victor Hugo, Joseph Méry, Rudyard Kipling)

Heaven will never be Heaven if my cats are not there to welcome me.
Unknown

How strange, how strange, how strange a tale! Look, a black cat with a tail.
Unknown

I figured we all started out as cats, but then the world put us on a leash and collar and turned us into dogs.
Unknown

I purr, therefore I am.
Unknown

If God created man in his own image, you've got to wonder in whose image did he create the cat, a more noble creature?
Unknown

If stretching meant wealth, the cat would be rich.
Unknown

If you want to know the character of a man, find out what his cat thinks of him.
Unknown

If you yell at a cat, you're the one who is making a fool of himself.
Unknown

In every cat there lies a guardian angel.
Unknown

In Paris during the winter solstice, the French are used to building a huge bonfire and place on top of it a cage in which they lock up a fox and two dozen cats before setting it on fire. They say King Francis does not consider it beneath him setting the cage on fire himself.
Unknown

In the eyes of cats, all things belong to them.
Unknown

It's in cat trees that you find kittens.
Unknown

It's really the cat's house - we are content to pay the rent.
Unknown

It's very hard to be polite if you're a cat.
Unknown

It wasn't curiosity that killed the cat; I did it with the lawnmower.
Unknown

My cat was bought in a ketchup.
Unknown

My husband said it was either him or the cat.. .I miss him sometimes.
Unknown

My little grandson is a darling, but he'll never take the place of my cats.
Unknown

On the eighth day God created the Cat.

Once upon a time a cat who prided herself on her wit and wisdom was prowling about the barn in search of food and saw a tail protruding from a hole. This is the appendage of a rat, she said to herself. Then she crept stealthily towards it and when she was within striking distance she made a jump at it and grasped it with her claws. Alas! It was not the appendage of a rat, but the tail of a snake, who whisked round and gave her a mortal bite.
Unknown

Purring is an automatic safety-valve device for dealing with excess of happiness.
Unknown

Rat got my tongue, said the Angora cat.
Unknown

Researchers have discovered that dogs can comprehend a vocabulary of 2,000 words, whereas cats can only comprehend 25 to 50. No one ever asked themselves how many words researchers can comprehend.
Unknown

Some people own cats and go on leading normal lives.
Unknown

The cat is mightily dignified until the dog comes along.
Unknown

The purity of a person's heart can be quickly assessed by the way he or she regards cats.
Unknown

There are many intelligent species in the universe. All are owned by cats.
Unknown

There is no snooze button on a cat who wants breakfast.
Unknown

Woman, cat and dog have fleas all along the year.
Unknown

Woman's knee, dog's nose, cat's paw: has there ever been anything so cold?
Unknown

Quotations by author

A real gentleman is the one who always calls a spade a spade, even if he stumbles on a cat and falls over.
Marcel Achard

I think all cats are wild. They act tamely only if there's a saucer of milk waiting for them.
Douglas Adams
Scott Adams

When the marmot plays or you caress it, its voice sounds like the murmur of a small dog or the purr of a cat.
Michel Adanson

A cat comes up when you call her - if she doesn't have anything better to do.
Bill Adler

In Egypt, cats... afford evidence that animal nature is not altogether intractable but that, when well-treated, animals are good at remembering kindness.
Aelian

The cat does not make you impure nor does it sully your water for ablutions.
Aisha, the wife of the Prophet

Cats are successful underachievers. They only need to purr in order to get free food and TLC. What other creature can lie around the house doing nothing beyond purring, and still get free food and TLC?
Jim Aites

There is no man for man: we are lying in wait for each other, like the cat for the mouse.
Mateo Aleman

Raton has nothing to fear for his paws, and there is no such fuss about the little trick he has done.
Jean le Rond d'Alembert

If the pull of the outside world is strong, there is also a pull towards the human. The cat may disappear on its own errands, but sooner or later, it returns once again for a little while, to greet us with its own type of love. Independent as they are, cats find more than pleasure in our company.
Lloyd Alexander

The cat liked to peep into the refrigerator and risked having his head caught by the closing door. He also climbed on to the top of the stove, discontinuing the practice after he singed his tail.

Lloyd Alexander

When you see a cat's paw lightly wash his pink nose and smooth his hair so fine, then fraternally embrace this feline.
Alphonse Allais

In the midst of a world that has always been a bit mad, the cat walks about with confidence.
Rosanne Amberson

One of the ways in which cats show happiness is by sleeping.
Cleveland Amory

And the cat said:
– Can you arch your back, or purr?
– No
– So, don't express absurd opinions when sensible people are talking.
Andersen

When a man smells of myrrh, his wife is a kitten to him.
When a man is suffering, his wife is a lioness to him.
Ankhsheshonq

A cat killed without any real desire.
It was a very rich cat and was not really hungry.
Jean Anouilh

I want in my house
A woman with her reason,
A cat weaving among books,
Friends in all seasons
Whom I cannot live without.
Guillaume Apollinaire

Some see "God" as "dog" spelled backwards. I see "God" as "cat" spelled with a vivid imagination.
Jacob Appel

The Siamese cat leapt silently and rubbed against one of the bare feet.
Louis Aragon

Female cats are very lascivious and make advances to male cats.
Aristote

The Dog and the Cat.
An open foe I much prefer
To a dear friend that scratches.
Arnadlt

Doc, there were four rats in this cage when I changed my bulbs. And now there are only three. Upon reflection, I think rat n° 4 must be located inside this cat.
Jack Arnold

When my teeth are not threatened, all the cats in the world are not dangerous.
Antonin Artaud

Indifferent to his past, careless of his future, the cat that has nine lives, more or less, has naturally increased in numbers despite the abuse he has suffered.
Yann Arthus-Bertrand

The cat sleeps on the sheik's lap and is at home on the prayer carpet.
Attar

Cats can be very funny, and have the oddest ways of showing they're glad to see you. Rudimac always peed in our shoes.
W. H. Auden

When I wake my cat up, he seems as grateful as one who is given the opportunity to sleep again.
Michel Audiard

At dusk, to dogs and wolves, all cats are grey.
Yvan Audouard

Dear friends, we've had our share of sorrow and joy this year. Troubles first. Our little cat Snowball was run over by a car. He went to kitty paradise. But we bought a new little cat, Snowball II, life goes on.
Véronique Augereau

We could see all around the stories of the most famous cats: Robillardus hung upside down on the board of rats, Puss- in- Boots Marquis de Carabas, the Cat who writes, the Cat who became a woman, the witches who became cats, the Sabbath and all its ceremonies.
Madame d'Aulnoy

Life is life - whether in a cat, a dog or man. There is no difference there between a cat and a man. The idea of such a difference is man's conception - to his own advantage.
Sri Aurobindo

Concerning an incomprehensible poem or a finely insignificant novel, he usually said that it was mush for cats.
Marcel Aymé

A cat will never drown if she sees the shore.
Francis Bacon

After her children have married, a mother occupies herself with raising cats.
Ahmad Bahgat

I remember that in my early childhood I used to fast, and whenever fasting was over I would go out taking my meal with me and give it to the stray dogs and cats.
Ahmad Bahgat

When cats aren't in, mice can dance.
Jean Antoine de Baïf

Cats are notoriously sore losers. Coming in second best, especially to someone as poorly coordinated as a human being, grates on their feelings.
Stephen Baker

Most beds sleep up to six cats. Even ten cats - without the owner.
Stephen Baker

By dint of being whipped, I realized that external cleanliness should be under an English Pussy.
Honoré de Balzac

Sky is in her eyes, hell is in her heart.
Honoré de Balzac

A dog, a cat is a heart with hair around.
Brigitte Bardot

If God is everywhere, the door that opens onto him is everywhere: the rose, the little cat, the morning stars. But the door closest to man is man.

_ *My name is Smokey, said the cat.*
_ *This is not a name, I'll call you Gri-Gri...*
_ *As you wish. Anyway, I never come when I'm called.*
René Barjavel

Surely the cat, when it assumes the meat loaf position and gazes meditatively through slitted eyes, is pondering thoughts of utter profundity...
Mij Colson Barnum

Dogs have owners, cats have staff.
Dave Barry

If I die before my cat, I want a I few of my ashes put in his food so I can live inside him.
Drew Barrymore

A cat is a free being. And ever so full of love. It's hard not to envy a cat.
Henri Bates

There's no need for a piece of sculpture in a home that has a cat.
Wesley Bates

Breeding purebred cats is like searching for perfection
Melissa Bateson

Both ardent lovers and austere scholars
Love in their mature years
The strong and gentle cats, pride of the house,
Who, like them, are sedentary and sensitive to cold.
Charles Baudelaire

The majority of people who still have back doors don't let their cats go out or come in through them.
Charlene Beane

Wilt thou, my Rosinette
Go shopping
For the King of husbands?
I'm not Tircis;
But in the shade of night,
I am still worth my price
And when it is dark
The most beautiful cats are gray.
Beaumarchais

Sorry, excuse me, she said, I can't find the concierge. It's for cutting a cat.
Simone de Beauvoir

To some extent, a cat could be another me or, better, a master model.
Béatrix Beck

Any household with at least one feline member has no need for an alarm clock.
Louise A. Belcher

Small nose, small teeth
Eyes that were not too eager
But where the blue pupil
Imitates the various color
Seen in this rainbow
that curves through the sky.
Joachim du Bellay

The cat is Parisian, the cat is a senior executive, the cat looks at Ségolène, the cat is bobo, the cat is Libé.
Zysla Belliat

You are my cat and I am your human.
Hilaire Belloc

I think it rather fine, this necessity for the tense bracing of the will before anything worth doing can be done. I rather like it myself. I feel it to be the chief thing that differentiates me from the cat by the fire.
Arnold Bennett

Happiness is like a cat, if you try to coax it or call it, it will avoid you; it will never come. But if you pay no attention to it and go about your business, you'll find it rubbing against your legs and jumping into your lap.
William John Bennett

A Swiss guard, smiling, said, «My Eminence, see, cats mount an assault on the holy seat."
To which Ratzinger replied "oh it does not seem that they are really so dangerous."
Benedict XVI

He lives in half light ,in secret places, free and alone - this mysterious little great being whom his mistress calls 'My cat.'
Margaret Benson

As every cat owner knows, nobody owns a cat.
Ellen Perry Berkeley

He (Benedict XVI) speaks with them, neither in German nor Italian, but using a particular and transcendent language and the felines who listen charm him.
Monseigneur Bertone

Cats, small or big, are perhaps the most beautiful creatures on this earth.
Claire Bessant

Well, says Love hiding in paradox, what is a lover? It is an instrument which is rubbed to have fun. Cuvier said to me: "Your cat does not caress you, it caresses itself against you."
Henri Beyle (Stendhal)

Purring is the cat's smile.
Hector Bianciotti

Cat: A soft, indestructible automaton provided by nature to be kicked when things go wrong in the domestic circle.
Ambrose Bierce

I called my cat William because no shorter name fits the dignity of his character. Poor old boy, he has fits now, so I call him Fitz-William.
Josh Billings

At the peak of heat in summer months, [...] the cat remains dry and cold. A cat will not stay with a man, except the one who feeds him.
Hildegarde de Bingen

Better feed one's mind than Siamese cats.
Francis Blanche

Cats have brushed against my ankle on crossing my way for so long that my gait, both at home and out of doors, has been compared to that of a man wading through low surf.
Roy Blount, Jr.

Dogs come when they're called. Cats take the message and call you back
Mary Bly

A Mouse is afraid of cats, a cat is afraid of dogs.
Christian Bobin

Cats' love is the first step towards aesthetics.
Isabelle Bonte

The name of the god who guards you is Cat.
The Book of the Dead

A man who was loved by 300 women singled me out to live with him. Why? I was the only one without a cat.
Elayne Boosler

He is a cat, therefore he is free.
Gilbert Bordes

They fear that some beings more powerful than themselves - dogs or humans – could cause them some damage or some injury.
Mikhaïl Boulgakov

Animals were created by God to give men a sense of superiority.
Philippe Bouvard

Cats are creatures that express a multitude of moods and attitudes.
Karen Brademeyer

If you are too gentle with a cat who lives with you, he looks like fanning himself and has a distant look, like those bitches of yore who seemed to say: Come on, speak by all means, I'm not concerned.
Pierre Brasseur

Adopted in Japan by the imperial family at the end of the first millennium, the cat became the ancestor of Maneki Neko, a small white cat statuette sitting with one leg lifted, which is found in much of Asia where it is a sign of happiness.
Raymonde Branger

When George in Pudding time came o'er,
And Moderate Men looked big, Sir,
My Principles I chang'd once more,
And so became a Whig, Sir.
Vicar of Bray

*It is a cat of ill fortune
A poor alley cat
Having tamed me
He did not teach me
only good manners
so as to be a good cat.*

Marcel Bréchet

The little cat is dead, Sunda Muscat does not make them sing anymore.

Jacques Brel

We brought with us a cat in the ship, a most amicable cat and greatly loved by us; but he grew to a monstrous size through the eating of fish.

St Brendan

We'll have one day to make up our minds and call a spade a spade and bus stoning an act of urban terrorism.

Alexis Brezet

A cat isn't fussy--just so long as you remember he likes his milk in the shallow, rose-patterned saucer and his fish on the blue plate. From which he will pick it, and eat it off the floor.

Arthur Bridges

I can say with sincerity that I love cats. A cat is an animal that has more human feelings than anyone else.

Emilie Brontë

A cat is nobody's fool.

Heywood Brown

A cat can maintain a position of curled up somnolence in your lap until you are nearly upright. At the last minute she hopes your conscience will get the better of you and you will sit down again.

Pam Brown

Cats can work out mathematically exactly where to sit so as to cause most inconvenience.

Pam Brown

The cat has been described as the most perfect animal, the acme of muscular perfection and the supreme example in the animal kingdom of the coordination of mind and muscle.

Roseanne Ambrose Brown

In order to keep a true perspective of one's importance, everyone should have a dog that will worship him and a cat that will ignore him.

Dereke Bruce

When you are looking at it, a cat acts like a princess, but the very minute it thinks you are not looking, a cat acts like a fool.
KC Buffington

Nothing on earth could keep any cats a moment longer in a place where they would not want to be.
Georges Louis Leclerc, comte de Buffon

Prowling about his own quiet backyard or lying asleep by the fire, he is still only a whisker away from the wilds.
Jean Burden

I love cats. I even think we have one at home.
Edward L Burlingame

Hatred of the cat reflects a spirit ugly, stupid, boorish, bigoted.
William Seward Burroughs

The message of the cauda equina is that either you're driving a cement mixer or doing the kitty litter and neither one nor the other inspires an erection.
Gérard Butler

I must have a cat whom I 'll find homeless, wandering about the courtyard, and to whom, therefore, I will be under no obligation. I have already selected a dirty little drunken wretch of a kitten to be the successor to my poor old cat.
Samuel Butler

If we treated everyone we meet with the same affection we bestow upon our favourite cat, they, too, would purr.
Martin Buxbaum

To err is human, to purr is feline.
Robert Byrne

Personally, I would not give a fig for any man's religion from which horse, cat and dog would not draw any benefits. Life in any form is our perpetual responsibility.
S. Parkes Cadman

Her name means "cat" and "light" in Egyptian. Descending probably from a subspecies of spotted African wild cats, our superb Mau was domesticated in ancient Egypt and was made the object of true worship.

Impossible not to mention, almost in spite of oneself, the little cat who sleeps at the light junction of these lines of lingerie.
Louis Calaferte

She had a swan's neck, a cat's eyes, an eagle's gaze, a wasp's waist, a gazelle's legs, a lion's temperament, a dog's character. Yet, she was a woman.
Louis Calaferte

It was the heart of summer when, on hot rooftops, cats were making love to their females trembling like women. Love with cries of love.
Henri Calet

The city of cats and the city of men exist one inside the other, but they are not the same city.
Italo Calvino

When the barometer washes itself behind its ears, the cat forecasts rain.
Léo Campion

The cats raised their eyes pale with sleep, without yet stirring
Albert Camus

A cat determined not to be found can fold itself up like a pocket handkerchief if it wants to.
Louis Camuti

Cats don't like change without their consent.
Roger A. Caras

Cats fear water, so they prefer sunbathing.
Stéphane Caron

In every kennel there sleeps a dog.
Gilles Carrez

Cats always know whether people like or dislike them. They do not always care enough to do anything about it.
Winifred Carriere

The dog growls when it's angry and wags its tail when happy. I growl when I'm pleased and wag my tail when I am angry. So I'm mad! (Cheshire cat).
Lewis Carroll

In the Middle Ages, cats and cat women were regarded as evil. Nonsense, of course, witches were just single, independent women who broke society's rules
Catwoman

Those who will play with cats must expect to be scratched.
Miguel de Cervantes

A drowsing little cat is an image of perfect beatitude.
Jules Champfleury (Jules Husson)

Do not think he caresses you, he caresses himself.

                                      Chamfort

Of all domestic animals the cat is the most expressive. His face is capable of showing a wide range of expressions. His tail is a mirror of his mind. His gracefulness is surpassed only by his agility. And, along with all this, he has a sense of humor.
                                     Walter Chandoha

Old ma Michel lost her cat
[...]
Your cat will be sold as a rabbit!
                                                   Chanson

Two things are aesthetically perfect in the world - the clock and the cat.
                            Emile-Auguste Chartier (Alain)

There is something of the camel about cats
                                         R. Chartrand

What I like in the cat is this independent almost ungrateful character that makes him focus on nobody, and the indifference with which he can go from living rooms to native alleys.
               François René, vicomte de Chateaubriand

Let take a cat, and fostre him wel with milk, And tendre flesh, and make his couche of silk, And let him seen a mous go by the wal; Anon he weyveth milk, and flesh, and al, And every deyntee that is in that hous, Swich appetyt hath he to ete a mous.
                                   Geoffrey Chaucer

But nature does not say that cats are more valuable than mice; nature makes no remark on the subject. She does not even say that the cat is enviable or the mouse pitiable. We think the cat superior because we have (or most of us have) a particular philosophy to the effect that life is better than death. But if the mouse were a German pessimist mouse, he might not think that the cat had beaten him at all. He might think he had beaten the cat by getting to the grave first.
                             Gilbert Keith Chesterton

Someone really superstitious is one who is convinced that passing under a black cat brings bad luck.
                                     Jean-Loup Chiflet

I hate you, your house smells of cat piss! Why do all the houses of drug dealers smell of cat piss?
                                      Margaret Cho

A green light shone in her eyes. Eyes that looked like a cat's.
                                       Agatha Christie

All dogs look up to you. All cats look down on you. Only the pig looks at you as an equal.
Winston Churchill

*The Cat goes out
And the cat comes back
And no one can follow her
Upon her track.
She knows where she's going
She knows where she's been, all we can do
Is to let her in.*
Marchette Chute

Even the stupidest cat seems to know more than any dog.
Eleanor Clark

Every cat is special in its own way.
Sara Jane Clark

It is often said that the domestic cat is an exploiter of humans rather than the other way round. This is because he cat's solitary nature, demanding personality and secret night life set it apart from all other domestic animals.
Juliet Clutton-Brock

If I prefer cats to dogs, this is because there is no police cat.
Jean Cocteau

All cats speak French.
Sidonie Gabrielle Claudine Colette

While cats enjoyed their favourite virtual fantasies, mice were able to exploit the planet and live up to the full in the real world as in a big cheese.
Eoin Colfer

This cat may be the only witness to this horrible crime. I want this cat.
Colombo

It is easier to have relations with a poor cat than with a rich man.
Coluche

No tame animal has lost less of its native dignity or maintained more of its ancient reserve. The domestic cat might rebel tomorrow.
William Conway

A cat cares for you only as a source of food, security, and a place in the sun. Her high self-sufficiency is her charm.
Charles Horton Cooley

I never married because there was no need. I have three pets at home which answer the same purpose as a husband. I have a dog

which growls every morning, a parrot which swears all afternoon, and a cat that comes home late at night.
Marie Corelli

Any conditioned cat-hater can be won over by any cat who chooses to make the effort.
Paul Corey

Cats are designated friends.
Norman Corwin

I'm aloof, I like to run around outside, but I also like to curl up in warm spots. I eat fish.
Megan Coughlin

What if it was cats who had invented technology? Would they have tv shows starring rubber squeak toys?
Douglas Coupland

If a cat does something, we call it instinct; if we do the same thing, for the same reason, we call it intelligence.
Will Cuppy

Cats come and go without ever leaving.
Martha Curtis

The cat has always been associated with the moon. Like the moon it comes to life at night, escaping from humanity and wandering over housetops with its eyes beaming out through the darkness.
Patricia Dale-Green

The grammarian ibn Babshad was sitting with his friends on the roof of a mosque in Cairo, eating some food. When a cat passed by, they gave her some morsels: she took them and ran away, only to come back time and time again. The scholars followed her and saw her running to an adjacent house on whose roof a blind cat was sitting. The cat carefully placed the morsels in front of her. Babshad was so moved by God's caring for the blind creature that he gave up all his belongings and lived in poverty, completely trusting in God until he died in 1067.
Damiri

I have an Egyptian cat. He leaves a pyramid in every room.
Rodney Dangerfield

To respect the cat is the beginning of the aesthetic sense.
Erasmus Darwin

A mathematician is a blind man in a dark room looking for a black cat which isn't there.
Charles Darwin

Perhaps God made cats so that man might have the pleasure of fondling the tiger...
Robertson Davies

Way down deep, we're all motivated by the same urges. Cats have the courage to live by them.
Jim Davis (Garfield)

A common cat is worth four legal pence...
Hywel Dda

A cat with kittens nearly always decides sooner or later to move them.
Sidney Denham

*Prince, often we deliberate,
But we can say, like the rat
About advice that fails:
Who will hang the bell to the cat's tail?*
Eustache Deschamps

When a cat chooses to be friendly, it's a big deal, because a cat is picky.
Mike Deupree

If he is comical, it is only because of the incongruity of so demure a look and so wild a heart.
Alan Devoe

Cats look beyond appearances - beyond species entirely, it seems - to peer into the heart.
Barbara L. Diamond

What greater gift than the love of a cat?
Charles Dickens

You remember my ideal cat always has a huge rat in its mouth, just going out of sight - though going out of sight holds a peculiar pleasure of its own.
Emily Dickinson

There are cats and cats.
Denis Diderot

Everybody wants to be a Cat.
Walt Disney

Some people say that cats are sneaky, evil, and cruel. True, and they have many other fine qualities as well.
Missy Dizick

Actually, cats do this to protect you from gnomes who come and steal your breath while you sleep.
John Dobbin

There are people who reshape the world by force or argument, but the cat just lies there, dozing, and the world quietly reshapes itself to suit his comfort and convenience.
Allen and Ivy Dodd

Some people are uncomfortable with the idea that humans belong to the same class of animals as cats and cows and raccoons. They're like the people who become successful and then don't want to be reminded of the old neighborhood.
Phil Donahue

Cats seem to have an innate understanding of the pleasures of life that humans often forget. We can learn a lot by closely observing our feline friends.
Glenn Dromgoole

One of the quickest routes to a cat's brain is through its stomach.
Ian Dunbar

Many cats simply pounce only on their own drummers.
Karen Duprey

No amount of time can erase the memory of a good cat, and no amount of masking tape can ever totally remove his fur from your couch.
Leo Dworken

If a homeless cat could talk, it would probably say, 'Give me shelter, food, companionship and love, and I will be yours for life!
Susan Easterly

In the beginning, God created man, but seeing him so feeble, He gave him the cat.
Warren Eckstein

Curiosity is the very basis of education and if you tell me that curiosity killed the cat, I'll only say the cat died nobly.
Arnold Edinborough

People that don't like cats haven't met the right one yet.
Deborah A. Edwards

To my mind here is nothing in the animal world, more delightful than grown cats at play. They are so swift and light and graceful, so subtle and designing, and yet so richly comical.
Monica Edwards

You see, the wire telegraph is a kind of a very, very long cat. You pull his tail in New York and his head is mewing in Los Angeles. Do you understand this? And the radio operates exactly the same way: you send signals here, they receive them there. The only difference is that there is no cat.

Albert Einstein

Cats don't bark – and consumers today don't salivate on command as they seemed to do a couple of decades ago. Consumers today behave more like cats than Pavlov's pooch. Times have changed – and so have we probably.
Bryan Eisenberg

Animals are such agreeable friends - they ask no questions, they pass no criticism.
George Eliot

When you see a cat in deep meditation, the reason, I tell you, is always the same: his mind is lost in bottomless contemplation. At the thought of the thought of the thought of his name: Mysterious and inaccessible Singular Name.
Thomas Stearns Eliott

Again I must remind you that a dog's a dog - a cat's a cat.
Thomas Stearns Eliott

Macavity, Macavity, there's no one like Macavity, there never was a cat of such deceitfulness and suavity.
Thomas Stearns Eliott

Do you see that kitten chasing her own tail so prettily? If you could look with her eyes, you might see her surrounded with hundreds of figures performing complex dramas, with tragic and comic issues, long conversations, many characters, many ups and downs of fate.
Ralph Waldo Emerson

A cat is the only domestic animal I know who washes its hindquarters and does a damned impressive job of it.
Joseph Epstein

O cat of lapis lazuli, great of forms… mistress of the embalming house, grant peace to the beautiful West.
Papyrus d'Espaheran

I was only a small child when the seeds of cat enchantment were sown within me.
May Eustace

Some cats are blind and stone deaf but ain't no cat wuz ever dumb.
Anthony Henderson Euwer

My sorrows will be over when I find companionship in a cat.
Ahmad ibn Faris

It always gives me a shiver when I see a cat seeing what I can't see.
Eleanor Farjeon

A sturdy lad… who teams it, farms it… and always like a cat falls on his feet, is worth a hundred of these city dolls.

Marsilio Ficino

Almost everybody can be imagined as either a cat or a dog.
F. Scott Fitzgerald

When you're special to a cat, you're special indeed... she brings to you the gift of her preference of you, the sight of you, the sound of your voice, the touch of your hand.
Leonore Fleisher

The cat in gloves catches no mice.
Benjamin Franklin

Four little Persians, but only one looked in my direction. I extended a tentative finger and two soft paws clung to it. There was a contented sound of purring, I suspect, on both parts.
George Freedley

I rarely meddled in the cat's personal affairs and she rarely meddled in mine. Neither of us was foolish enough to attribute human emotions to our pets.
Kinky Friedman

The smart cat doesn't let anyone know who he is.
H.G. Frommer

Nothing's more playful than a young cat, nor graver than an old one.
Thomas Fuller

The cat dropped the rat between its two front paws. There are those, it said with a sigh, in tones as smooth as oiled silk, who have suggested that the tendency of a cat to play with its prey is a merciful one - after all, it permits the occasional funny running little snack to escape, from time to time. How often does your dinner manage to escape?
Neil Gaiman

Everything a cat is and does physically is to me beautiful, lovely, stimulating, soothing, attractive and an enchantment.
Paul Gallico

The mice which find themselves helplessly caught between a cat's teeth acquire no merit from their enforced sacrifice.
Mohandas Mahatma Gandhi

Don't think that I'm silly for liking it, I just happen to like the simple little things, and I love cats!
Michelle Gardner

Poets generally love cats – because poets have no delusions about their own superiority.
Marion Garretty

Her function is to sit and be admired.
Georgina Strickland Gates

If you are worthy of its affection, a cat will be your friend, but never your slave.
Théophile Gautier

A cat is a hand-fed tiger.
Vakaoka Genrin

Cats know how to obtain food without labour, shelter without confinement, and love without penalties.
Walter Lionel George

Cats are the ultimate narcissists. You can tell this by all the time they spend on personal grooming. Dogs aren't like this. A dog's idea of personal grooming is to roll himself over a dead fish.
James Gorman

He has become a much better cat than I a person. Hs gentle urgings made me realize that life doesn't end just because one has a few obstacles to overcome.
Mary F. Graf

Do not meddle in the affairs of cats, for they are subtle and will piss on your computer.
Bruce Graham

Prose books are the show dogs I breed and sell to support my cat.
Robert Graves

After scolding one's cat one looks into its face and is seized by the ugly suspicion that it understood every word. And has filed it for reference.
Charlotte Gray

Any cat who misses a mouse pretends it was aiming at the dead leaf.
Charlotte Gray

All cats like being the focus of attention.
Peter Gray

Cats are kind masters, just as long as you remember your station.
Paul Gray

What female heart can despise gold? What cat's averse to fish?
Thomas Gray

There is, incidentally, no way of talking about cats that enables one to come off as a sane person.
Dan Greenberg

If your cat favours its left paw, chances are that it possesses psychic ability to some extent.

Dr. David Greene

In performing a variety of intellectually demanding tasks, cats usually emerge as clear winners (over dogs).

Dr. David Greene

Fans think they want to see more than the 10 to 20 seconds of Itchy and Scratchy that we put in on the show, but my feeling is that less is more. Once you've skinned and flayed a cat, ripped his head off, made him drink acid and tied his tongue to the moon, there really isn't that much to say.

Matt Groening

He was lost! not a shade of doubt as to that;
For he never barked at a slinking cat.

Arthur Guiterman

Cat lovers can readily be identified. Their clothes always look old and worn. Their sheets look like bath towels and their bath looks like a collection of knitting mistakes.

Eric Gurney

A Half-god himself, he attracted Pharaoh. No doubt he knows how to seduce you now.

Didier Hallépée

Sleeping is a little bit like dying.
No matter since I have nine lives!

Didier Hallépée

Deep through his enigmatic gaze, 40 centuries of feline friendship look down on you.

Didier Hallépée

You may have a cat in the room with you with no anxiety about anything except eatables. The presence of a cat is positively soothing to a student.

Philip Gilbert Hamerton

Which is more beautiful - feline movement or feline stillness?

Elizabeth Hamilton

What's virtue in a man can't be virtue in a cat.

Gail Hamilton

Cats are much like what they used to be when they were first domesticated. They are very independent because they had to be in order to survive.

Dr. Raymond Hampton

You never saw such a crazy cat. 'Up the wall' took on a literal meaning with him.

Arnold Hano

Who hath a better friend than a cat?
William Hardwin

In my days, we didn't have dogs or cats. All I had was Silver Beauty, my beloved paper clip.
Jennifer Hart

Anyone who considers protocol unimportant has never dealt with a cat.
Robert A. Heinlein

One cat just leads to another.
Ernest Hemingway

A cat is a pygmy lion who loves mice, hates dogs, and patronizes human beings.
Oliver Herford

Cats are connoisseurs of comfort.
James Herriot

A cat doesn't know what it wants and wants more of it.
Richard Hexem

A woman hath nine lives like a cat.
Georges Heywood

When all candles be out, all cats be gray.
John Heywood

If your cat falls from a tree, go indoors and have a good laugh.
Patricia Hitchcock

There are few things in life more heartwarming than to be welcomed by a cat.
Tay Hohoff

There is no cat 'language'. Painful as it is for us to admit, they don't need one.
Barbara Holland

Essentially, you do not so much teach your cat as bribe him.
Lynn Hollyn

I have noticed that what cats appreciate most in a human being is not his or her ability to produce food, which they take for granted--but his or her entertainment value.
Geoffrey Household

It doesn't do to be sentimental about cats; the best ones won't respect you for it.
Susan Howatch

The way to keep a cat is to try to chase it away.

Cats at firesides live luxuriously and are the picture of comfort.
Leigh Hunt

God made the cat so that man might have the pleasure of caressing the tiger.
Victor Hugo

If you want to write, keep cats.
Aldous Huxley

Cat, I'm a kitty-cat, and I dance, dance, dance, and I dance, dance, dance
Steve Ibsen

A cat who turns her nose up at bread does not deserve meat.
Mehmet Ildan

A cat can be trusted to purr when she is pleased, which is more than can be said for human beings.
William Ralph Inge

Cats are glorious creatures who must on no account be underestimated
Their eyes are fathomless depths of cat-world mysteries.
Lesley Anne Ivory

A cat's got her own opinion of human beings. She doesn't say much, but can tell you enough to make you anxious not to hear the whole of it.
Jérôme Klapka Jérôme

Hang sorrow, care'll kill a cat.
Ben Jonson

The domestic cat seems to have greater confidence in itself than in anyone else.
Lawrence N. Johnson

His friendship is not easily won but it is something worth having.
Michael Joseph

I cannot deny that a cat lover and his cat have a master/slave relationship. The cat is the master.
Arthur R. Kassin

Cats and mongooses will be used as protection against rats and snakes.
Kautilya (Arthashastra)

Whoever has stolen or killed a small animal (rooster, cat, dog, pig) of a value under 25 panas will have the nose cut or pay a fine of 54 panas.
Kautilya (Arthashastra)

Their uncanny intelligence, a strong streak of stubbornness and independence can make it a challenge to show them. If you wish to show a Mau, you must begin early when it is a kitten, getting it acclimatized to the sights and sounds of a cat show, otherwise they may decide they don't like the whole idea of leaving home when they are older. It's their stubbornness coming through!
Dee Keenan

Cats are intended to teach us that not everything in nature has a function.
Garrison Keillor

It is good to look at things from different perspectives. However, never at your exact opposite, that is your reflection in the mirror of whom you will never be the winner. As any cat can tell you.
Frederik Kerling

Women are like cats and dogs. If you can attract any cat and make any dog listen to you, you can have any women you like.
Frederik Kerling

Mewing is like aloha - it can mean anything.
Hank Ketchum

Curiosity killed the cat and information brought it back!
Marian Keyes

He turned his back on me and roared away, like a cat showing me its bum.
Marian Keyes

Cat said, 'I am not a friend, and I am not a Servant. I am the Cat who walks by himself, and I wish to come into your Cave.'
Rudyard Kipling

Cats are rather delicate creatures and they are subject to a good many ailments, but I never heard of one who suffered from insomnia.
Joseph Wood Krutch

Cats seem to act on the principle that it never does any harm to ask for what you want.
Joseph Wood Krutch

A dog is like a liberal, he wants to please everybody. A cat doesn't really need to know that everybody loves him.
William Kunstler

No favour can win gratitude from a cat.
Jean de La Fontaine

I put down my book, The Meaning of Zen, and see the cat smiling into her fur as she delicately combs it with her rough pink tongue. Cat, I would lend you this book to study but it appears you have already

read it. She looks up and gives me her full gaze. Don't be ridiculous, she purrs, I wrote it.
Dilys Laing

Cats, like men, are flatterers.
Walter Savage Landor

Of all animals, the cat alone attains to contemplative life. He regards the wheel of existence from without, like the Buddha.
Andrew Lang

The cat could very well be man's best friend but would never stoop to admitting it.
Doug Larson

Oh, Auntie, isn't he a beauty! And is he a gentleman or a lady? Neither, my dear! I had him fixed. It saves him from so many undesirable associations.
D. H. Lawrence

The Owl and the Pussy-Cat went to sea in a beautiful pea-green boat. They took some honey, and plenty of money, wrapped up in a five-pound note.
Edward Lear

His mind is like a steel trap - full of mice.
Foghorn Leghorn

Cats are living adornments.
Edwin Lent

If a fish is the movement of water embodied, given shape, then a cat is a diagram and pattern of subtle air.
Doris Lessing

A dog thinks: Hey, these people I live with feed me, love me, provide me with a nice warm, dry house, pet me, and take good care of me... They must be Gods! A cat thinks: Hey, these people I live with feed me, love me, provide me with a nice warm, dry house, pet me, and take good care of me... I must be a God!
Ira Lewis

If there were an invisible cat in that chair, the chair would look empty; but the chair does look empty, therefore there is an invisible cat in it.
Jack Lewis

A cat's name may tell you more about its owners than it does about the cat.
Linda W. Lewis

I found out why cats drink out of the toilet. My mother told me it's because the water is cold in there. How did my mother know that?
Wendy Liebman

I care not much for the religion of a man whose dog and cat are not the better for it.
                                                Abraham Lincoln

The world has different owners at sunrise... Even your own garden does not belong to you. Rabbits and blackbirds have the lawns; a tortoise-shell cat who never appears in daytime patrols the brick walls, and a golden-tailed pheasant glints his way through the iris spears.
                                                Anne Lindbergh

I saw the most beautiful cat today. It was sitting by the side of the road, its two forepaws neatly and graciously put together. Then it gravely swished around its tail to completely encircle itself. It was so fit and beautifully neat, that gesture, and so self-satisfied, so complacent.
                                                Ann Morrow Lindbergher

The cat is a wild animal that inhabits the homes of humans.
                                                Konrad Lorenz

If by chance I seated myself to write, she very slyly, very tenderly, seeking protection and caresses, would softly take her place on my knee and follow the comings and goings of my pen -- sometimes effacing, with an unintentional stroke of her paw, lines of whose tenor she disapproved.
                                                Pierre Loti

In its flawless grace and superior self-sufficiency I have seen a symbol of the perfect beauty and bland impersonality of the universe itself, objectively considered, and in its air of silent mystery there resides for me all the wonder and fascination of the Unknown.
                                                Howard P. Lovecraft

In my opinion, one of the pleasures of cats' company is their devotion to bodily comfort.
                                                Sir Compton Mackenzie

There is no harm in forgetting for an hour or two the problems of poverty and children.
And forgetting the heat and flies…
And forgetting there is another world outside these bars…
And enjoying playing with a black cat.
                                                Naguib Mahfouz

The cat blinks. She has waited a long time for you to remember her name. Her purr, steady as the clock's heartbeat, is a bridge from the place you have left to the place where you now are. A reliable companion, she guides you towards the land whose name comes to your lips slowly.

Lisa Suhair Majaj

The modern Egyptian domestic cat, which one encounters in the cafes and bazaars, in the noisy streets of Cairo and in the dusty sun-drenched villages, is a graceful delicate little creature, usually much smaller than Western cats.

Jarovir Malek

I gave my cat a bath the other day... They love it. He sat there, he enjoyed it, it was fun for me. The fur would stick to my tongue, but other than that...

Steve Martin

Cats do not have to be shown how to have a good time, for they are unfailingly ingenious in that respect.

James Mason

The cat does not negotiate with the mouse.

Robert K. Massie

The acorn becomes an oak through automatic growth; no commitment is necessary. The kitten similarly becomes a cat out of pure instinct. Nature and being are identical in creatures like them. But a man or woman becomes fully human only by his or her choices and his or her commitment to them. People attain worth and dignity by the multitude of decisions they make from day to day. These decisions require courage.

Rollo May

A cat can purr its way out of anything.

Donna McCrohan

When your cat rubs the side of its face along your leg, it's affectionately marking you with its scent, identifying you as its private property, saying, in effect, 'You belong to me'.

Susan McDonough

The sun rose slowly, like a fiery fur ball coughed up uneasily onto a sky-blue carpet by a giant unseen cat.

Michael McGarel

Men need four things: food, shelter, a pussy and a strange pussy.

Jay McInernay

If there is one spot of sun spilling onto the floor, a cat will find it and soak it up.

Joan Asper McIntosh

A mew massages the heart.

Stuart McMillan

One of the oldest human needs is having someone to wonder where you are when you don't come home at night.

Margaret Mead

Women do not like timid men. Cats do not like prudent rats.
H.L. Mencken

Are cats lazy? Well, more power to them if they are. Which one of us has not entertained the dream of doing just as he likes, when and how he likes, and as much as he likes?
Fernand Mery

With their qualities of cleanliness, discretion, affection, patience, dignity, and courage, how many of us, I ask you, would be capable of becoming cats?
Fernand Mery

Cats are smart. You know it and I know it.
Debbie Mertens

Some animals are secretive; some are shy. A cat is private.
Leonard Michaels

A dog will flatter you but you have to flatter the cat.
George Mikes

When I raise a cat from kittenhood, it learns to read me so well that it can con me and predict what I'm going to do. A young adult cat doesn't know what to expect from me and I don't know what to expect from it, so we immediately have each other's attention.
Karl Lewis Miller

Cats regard people as warm-blooded furniture.
Jacquelyn Mitchard

Drenching the pavement, warming the wall, bathing the cat in a slumbering sprawl... Waking the buds that break from the tree. Shaking out gold, and all for free.
Tony Mitton

We cannot, unless we become cats, perfectly understand the cat's mind.
St. George Mivart

Cats Are Not impure; they keep watch about us.
The Prophet Mohammed

Kittens believe that all nature is occupied with diverting them.
F.A. Paradis de Moncrif

When the tea is brought in at five o'clock
And all the neat curtains are drawn with care,
The little black cat with bright green eyes
Suddenly starts purring there.
Harold Monro

When I play with my cat, who knows if I am not a pastime to her more than she is to me?
Michel Eyquem de Montaigne

At night all cats are grey.
Montluc

In my next life, I'd like to come back as a cat.
Patti J. Moran

The playful kitten with its pretty little tigerish gambol is infinitely more amusing than half the people one is obliged to live with in the world.
Lady Sydney Morgan

People with insufficient personalities are fond of cats. These people adore being ignored.
Henry Morgan

They are shoulder riders, refrigerator vultures, and AM "kissers" (furry alarm-clocks with warm raspy tongues.)
Melanie Morgan

His amiable amber eyes
Are very friendly, very wise;
Like Buddha, grave and fat,
He sits, regardless of applause,
And thinking, as he kneads his paws,
What fun to be a cat!"
Christopher Morley

Artists like cats; soldiers like dogs.
Desmond Morris

She rages like the goddess Sekhmet and she is friendly like the goddess Bastet.
The Myth of the Eye of the Sun

The trouble with a kitten is that eventually it becomes a cat.
Ogden Nash

The beasts of the desert shall drink from the river of Egypt and rest on its bank because nobody shall scare them away.
The Profecies of Nefertiti

Winners are different. They're a different breed of cat.
Byron Nelson

Cats do care. For example they know instinctively what time we have to be at work in the morning and they wake us up twenty minutes before the alarm goes off.
Michael Nelson

I have seen
How the cat trembles

*while sleeping
The night runs over him
like dark water*

                                                                             Pablo Neruda

I think I'll come back as a cat.

                                                                                 George Ney

A garden without cats, it will be generally agreed, can scarcely deserve to be called a garden at all.

                                                        Beverly Nichols

Man wishes woman to be peaceable, but in fact she is essentially warlike, like the cat.

                                              Friedrich Nietzsche

Most of us rather like our cats to have a streak of wickedness. I should not feel quite easy in the company of any cat that walked about the house with a saintly expression

                                                 Beverly Nichols

A cat is a puzzle for which there is no solution.

                                                Hazel Nicholson

My cat and I have an agreement: I leave her alone and don't make sudden moves when I wake up to find her perched on my chest, staring with an unblinking hostile gaze at my face and in return she rarely mutilates me.

                                                James Nicoll

Perhaps a child, like a cat, is so much inside himself that he does not see himself in the mirror.

                                                          Anais Nin

Cats like doors to be left open - in case they change their minds.

                                                 Rosemary Nisbet

Always the cat remains a little beyond the limits we try to set for him in our blind folly.

                                                André Norton

Another superiority of cat on man: he does not speak.

                                                Louis Nucera

Love plays with my heart as a cat plays with a mouse.

                                                Abu Nuwas

The white cat on the white chair lives white minutes I'm not even in.

                                             Naomi Shihab Nye

Cats possess so many of the same qualities as some people that it is often hard to tell people and cats apart.

                                                P. J. O'Rourke

To wake the sleeping cat.
Charles d'Orléans

The mathematical probability of a common cat doing exactly as it pleases is the one scientific absolute in the world.
Lynn M. Osband

The cat lets Man support her. But unlike the dog, she is no handlicker. Furthermore, unlike Man's other great good friend, the horse, the cat is no sweating serf of Man. The only labor she condescends to perform is to catch mice and rats, and that's fun.
Vance Packard

Our character is what God and cats know of us.
Thomas Paine

The last thing I would accuse a cat of is innocence.
Edward Paley

A baited cat may grow as fierce as a lion.
Samuel Palmer

Kittens believe that all nature is occupied with diverting them.
F.A. Paradis de Moncrif

You may not, cannot, appropriate beauty. It is the wealth of the eye, and a cat may gaze upon a king.
Theodore Parker

You cannot look at a sleeping cat and feel tense.
Jane Pauley

A dog is a dog, a bird is a bird, and a cat is a person.
Mugsy Peabody

Sleeping together is a euphemism for people, but tantamount to marriage with cats.
Marge Percy

A cat will do what it wants when it wants, and there's not a thing you can do about it.
Frank Perkins

The way to get on with a cat is to treat it as an equal - or even better, as the superior it knows itself to be.
Elizabeth Peters

A cat pours his body on the floor like water. It is restful just to see him.
William Lyon Phelps

God is really only another artist. He invented the giraffe, the elephant and the cat. He has no real style, he just goes on trying other things.
Pablo Picasso

I want to create a cat like the real cats I see crossing the streets, not like those you see in houses. They have nothing in common. The cat of the streets has bristling fur. It runs like a fiend, and if it looks at you, you think it is going to jump in your face.
Pablo Picasso

Managing senior programmers is like herding cats.
Dave Platt

Cats, too, with what silent stealthiness, with what light steps do they creep up to a bird!
Pline l'Ancien

It is told that in a cat's eyes, pupils fill and expand at full moon and contract on the wane of this star.
Plutarque

I wish I could write as mysteriously as a cat.
Edgar Allan Poe

I call a cat a cat and Rolet an impostor.
Jean-Baptiste Poquelin (Molière)

It's funny how dogs and cats know the inside of folks better than other folks do, isn't it?
Eleanor H. Porter

If cats could talk, they wouldn't.
Nan Porter

The problem with cats is that they have got exactly the same look whether they see a moth or a murderer with an axe.
Paula Poundstone

You can tell your cat anything and he'll still love you. If you lose your job or your best friend, your cat will think no less of you.
Helen Powers

In ancient times, cats were worshiped as gods. They have never forgotten this.
Terry Pratchett

Don't wake the sleeping cat.
Rabelais

They pissed everywhere!
Jean Racine

In reality, cats are probably better off remaining indoors and sending out their humans to deal with the outside world.
Dr. Phyllis Sherman Raschke

To go like a cat upon a hot bakestone.
Jean Ray

It is widely acknowledged that cats are akin to hackers.
Eric S. Raymond

Cats often devise their own sets of rules that they think we should live by, and they may be quick to chastise us if we fail to adhere to these rules!
Margaret Reister

She is told: "catch mice and leave birds!" This is very subtle and the sharpest cat may be mistaken.
Jules Renard

A kitten is chiefly remarkable for rushing about like mad at nothing whatever, and generally stopping before it gets there.
Agnès Repplier

People that hate cats will come back as mice in their next life.
Faith Resnick

Tibert the Cat: But do not forget it another time, cheats never win.
Reynard cycle

The cat in gloves catches no mice.
Franklin Delano Roosevelt

Even if you have just destroyed a Ming Vase, purr. Usually it will all be forgiven.
Lenny Rubenstein

Each one of our cats is a distinct, four-footed little person with an individual personality.
Ira B. Rubin

Rosebuds surrounded by thorns: Mother cat carrying babies in her mouth.
Rita Rudner

Cats are a waste of fur.
Jalaluddin Rumi

Dangling punch lines to forgotten stories remains in the language like the smile of the Cheshire cat.
William Safire

The cat is domestic only as far as suits its own ends…
Saki (H. H. Munro)

You may own a cat, but cannot govern one.
Kate Sanborn

When addressed, a gentleman cat does not move a muscle. He looks as if he hadn't heard.
Mary Sarton

My cat has got no name
We simply call him Cat;
He doesn't seem to blame
Anyone for that.

For he is not like us
Who often, I'm afraid,
Kick up quite a fuss
If our names are mislaid.

Vernon Scannell

Cats speak a subtle language in which few sounds carry many meanings, depending on how they are sung or purred. 'Mnrhnh' means comfortable soft chairs. It also means fish. It means genial companionship... and the absence of dogs.

Val Schaffner

When British naturalist E. W. Lane lived in Cairo in the 1830s he was quite amazed to see, every afternoon, a great number of cats gathering in the garden of the High Court, where people would bring baskets full of food for them. In this way, he was told, the qadi fulfilled obligations dating from the thirteen century-rule of the Mamluk sultan, al-Zahir Baybars,

Anne-Marie Schimmel

Because of our willingness to accept cats as superhuman creatures, they are the ideal animals with which to work creatively.

Roni Schotter

There are two sorts of refuge from the miseries of life: music and cats.

Albert Schweitzer

Cats are a mysterious kind of folk. There is more passing in their minds than we are aware of.

Walter Scott

There once were two men who went to a judge about a mother cat and her kitten which they both claimed to be theirs. The judge demanded that this cat be set free between their two houses and, depending on which one of the houses she chose, the chosen house would be her master's. And all the people got excited, and I got excited with them. But the cat did not go to either house.

Imam Shafi'i

Thrice the brinded cat hath mewed.

William Shakespeare

The cat will mew, and dog will have his day.

William Shakespeare

Many of us are like the little boy we met trudging along a country road with a cat-rifle over his shoulder. What are you hunting, buddy? we asked. Dunno, sir, I ain't seen it yet.

R. Lee Sharpe

One cat built a secret nest in my socks.
One sat in the window staring up at the street all day while we were at school.
One cat loved the radio dial.
One cat almost smiled

Naomi Shibab Nye

Cats don't adopt people. They adopt refrigerators.

Solomon Short

For every house is incomplete without him, and a blessing is lacking in the spirit.

Christopher Smart

Everything I know I learned from my cat: When you're hungry, eat. When you're tired, nap in a sunbeam. When you go to the vet's, pee on your owner.

Gary Smith

The Behaviour of men to animals and their behaviour to each other bear a constant relationship.

Herbert Spencer

In my next life I want to come back as one of my cats. They basically pretend we don't exist. They sit like two bumps on a log and watch us work for hours in the yard. They're probably wondering, along with the entire neighborhood, why we work so hard in our garden and it still looks like hell.

Annie Spiegelman

Who needs television when you have cats?

Lori Spigelmyer

Nothing is improved by anger, unless it be the arch of a cat's back.

Charles Haddon Spurgeon

Since each of us is blessed with only one life, why not live it with a cat?

Robert Stearns

My cat speaks sign language with her tail.

Robert A. Stern

Among animals, cats are the top-hated, frock-coated statesmen going about their affairs at their own pace.

Robert A. Stern

My name is Steven but they call me Cat.

Cat Stevens

You can give an order to a dog. To a cat, you can at most make a reasonable proposal.
Michael Stevens

It is in the nature of cats to do a certain amount of unescorted roaming.
Adlai Stevenson

When Mother Nature saw fit to remove the tail of the Manx, she left, in place of the tail, more cat.
Mary E. Stewart

I don't mind a cat, in its place. But its place is not right in the middle of my back at 4 a.m.
Maynard Good Stoddard

The artist is uncomfortable with his success and with the blizzard of fan mail it has produced. Kliban's recent collections have been conspicuously empty of cats. Cats are wonderful, Kliban once said. It's drawings of cats I'm getting tired of.
J. C. Suares

You can't own a cat. The best you can do is be partners.
Sir Harry Swanson

I know Sir John will go, though he was sure it would rain cats and dogs.
Jonathan Swift

It is in their eyes that their magic resides.
Arthur Symons

She has bewitched me with her darkness and light as she appears to be made of ebony and ivory.
Ibn Tabataba

I have studied many philosophers and many cats. The wisdom of cats is infinitely superior.
Hippolyte Taine

Dogs eat. Cats dine.
Ann Taylor

Cats, no less liquid than their shadows, offer no angles to the wind. They slip, diminished, neat, through loopholes lesser than themselves.
A. S. J. Tessimond

All cats love a cushioned couch.
Théocrite

One is never sure, watching two cats washing each other, whether it's affection, a taste for it, or a trial run for the jugular.
Helen Thomson

A cat sees no good reason why it should obey another animal, even if it does stand on two legs.
Sarah Thomson

It is not worth while going round the world to count the cats in Zanzibar.
Henry David Thoreau

Could the purr be anything but contemplative?
Irving Townsend

Fear is a slinking cat I find beneath the lilacs of my mind.
Sophie Tunnel

A man who carries a cat by the tail learns something he can learn in no other way.
Mark Twain

Cats are smarter than dogs. You cannot get eight cats to pull a sled through snow.
Jeff Valdez

A cat is never vulgar.
Carl Van Vechten

I believe cats to be spirits come to earth. A cat, I am sure, could walk on a cloud without going through.
Jules Verne

The smallest feline is a masterpiece.
Léonard de Vinci

A cat allows you to sleep on the bed. On the edge.
Jenny de Vries

Intelligence in the cat is underrated.
Louis Wain

If there was any petting to be done... he chose to do it. Often he would sit looking at me, and then, moved by a delicate affection, come and pull at my coat and sleeve until he could touch my face with his nose, and then go away contented.
Charles Dudley Warner

At Group L, Stoffel oversees six first-rate programmers, a managerial challenge roughly comparable to herding cats.
The Washington Post Magazine

I think one reason we admire cats, those of us who do, is their proficiency in one-upmanship. They always seem to come out on top,

no matter what they are doing--or pretend to do. Rarely do you see a cat discomfited. They have no conscience, and they never regret anything. Maybe we secretly envy them.
Barbara Webster

If I called her she would pretend not to hear, but would come a few moments later when it could appear that she had thought of doing so first.
Arthur Weigall

Cats are known to follow their own hidden purposes, did this this make of them, at the best, untrustworthily familiar?
Margaret Weis

The cat, which is a solitary beast, is single-minded and goes his way alone; but the dog, like his master, is confused in his mind.
H.G. Wells

In ancient times cats were worshipped as gods, this they have never forgotten.
Alfred North Whitehead

Recently we were discussing the possibility of making one of our cats Pope, and we decided that the fact she was not Italian and was a female, made the third point, her being a cat, irrelevant.
Katharine Whitehorn

Bathsheba! to whom no one ever said scat
No worthier cat
Ever sat on a mat,
Or caught a rat.
Requiescat!
John Whittier

A cat's behavior is a direct reflection of his feelings.
Carole Wilbourn

Like a graceful vase, a cat, even when motionless, seems to flow.
George F. Will

The phrase domestic cat is an oxymoron.
George F. Will

The final war will be between Pavlov's dog and Schrödinger's Cat.
Robert Anton Wilson

What is remarkable in cats is that the outer life they reveal to their masters is one of perpetual boredom.
Robley Wilson, Jr.

Women, poets, and especially artists, are like cats delicate natures who can only express their delicacy of feelings
Helen M. Winslow

When mom found my diaphragm, I told her it was a bathing cap for my cat.
Liz Winston

The best you can do is admire the cat's cradle, and maybe knot it up a bit more. History should be a hammock for swinging in and a toy for playing with, the way cats play. Claw it, chew it, rearrange it and at bedtime it's still a ball of string full of knots. Nobody should mind.
Jeanette Winterson

As a class, Cats have never completely got over the snootiness caused by that fact that in Ancient Egypt they were worshipped as gods.
P G Wodehouse

You can visualize a hundred cats. Beyond that, you can't. Two hundred, five hundred, it all looks the same.
Jack Wright

If Darwin's theory of evolution was correct, cats would by now be able to operate a can opener.
Larry Wright

Curiosity killed the cat, but for a while I was a suspect.
Steven Wright

No matter if it is a white cat or a black cat; as long as it can catch mice, it is a good cat.
Deng Xiaoping

Cats are oppressed, dogs terrify them, landladies starve them, boys stone them, everybody speaks of them with contempt. If they were human beings we could talk of their oppressors with a studied violence, add our strength to theirs, even organize the oppressed and like good politicians sell our charity for power.
William Butler Yeats

I could never understand that kitchen meat did not belong to cats.
Émile Zola

THE EGYPTIAN MAU ON THE WEB

The web is perpetually changing. We can't guarantee that these links will not have changed when you read this book.

This is not a definitive list of cat associations and Mau breeders. Appear here only those who had a web site when this book was first written.

In no case can we guarantee the quality of the breeders quoted here. Our quality criteria are those of AIME and some people may consider them as too rigorous.

Cats and Egypt

Cats and Egypt

in French and in English
http://egypt.fondcombe.com/

The Egyptian Mau clubs

Association Internationale du Mau Egyptien (AIME)

in 7 languages
http://aime.ws

Egyptian Mau Breeders' and Fanciers' Club (EMBFC)

in English
http://embfc.com

The Egyptian Mau Club

in English
http://www.egyptianmau.uk.co/

Global Egyptian Mau Society (GEMS)

in English
http://gemsclub.tripod.com

Egyptian Mau Enthusiasts (EME)

in English

The author's web site

Fondcombe Cattery

in 7 languages
http://fondcombe.com

The Egyptian Mau Forum

Maus d'Amour, the forum

in French and in English
http://forum.aime.ws

The Cat associations

European Cat Fancy

in English
http://www.eurocatfancy.org

Federazione Italiana Associazione Feline (FIAF)

in Italian
http://www.fiafonline.it/

Feline Fancier of Belgium

in English and in German
http://users.skynet.be/DVR-web/FFB/

Cat Friends of Germany e. V (CFG)

in English
http://www.catfriends.de/

Cat Fancier Association (CFA)

in English
http://www.cfainc.org/

American Cat Fancier Association (ACFA)

in English
mcats@bellsouth.net

The International Cat Association (TICA)

in English
http://www.tica.org/

American Association of Cat Enthusiasts (AACE)

in English
http://www.aaceinc.org/

Katz Incorporated – New Zealand (KATZ)

in English
http://catzinc.org.nz

The e-groups

EmauC
Home page   http://groups.yahoo.com/groups/EmauC
e-mail   EmauC@yahoogroups.com
Reserv to members

EMBFC
Home page   http://groups.yahoo.com/groups/EMBFC
e-mail   EMBFC@yahoogroups.com
Reserv to members

MauCats
Home page   http://groups.yahoo.com/groups/MauCats
e-mail   MauCats@yahoogroups.com
Open to all

Mau-of-Egypt
Home page   http://groups.yahoo.com/groups/Mau-of-Egypt
e-mail   Mau-of-Egypt@yahoogroups.com
Open to all

G-E-M-S
Home page   http://groups.yahoo.com/groups/G-E-M-S
e-mail   G-E-M-S@yahoogroups.com
Reserved to members

maugang
Home page   http://groups.yahoo.com/groups/maugang
e-mail   maugang@yahoogroups.com
Reserved to members

egyptianmaus
Home page   http://groups.yahoo.com/groups/egyptianmaus
e-mail   egyptianmaus@yahoogroups.com
Open to all

rizykitty
Home page   http://groups.yahoo.com/groups/rizzykitty
e-mail   rizzykitty@yahoogroups.com
Open to all

Miscellaneous

<u>Dr Susan Little's website</u>
Vet information for Cat breeders and fanciers

In English
http://www.catvet.homestead.com

<u>Gianfranco Montovani home page</u>
Paintings of animals made by Gianfranco Montovani, international feline judge

In Italian
http://digilander.libero.it/gfmantovani/index.html

<u>Bastet</u>
Website dedicated to Bastet Godness

In English
http://inanna.virtualave.net/bastet.html

<u>Glossaire félin</u>
http://dolores.bauchet.free.fr/glossaire.htm

In French
French dictionnary of feline vocabulary

<u>Egyptian Name translator</u>
Translator in hieroglyphs

In English
http://www.eyelid.co.uk/e-name.htm

Nom en hiéroglyphes

Translator in hieroglyphs

In French
http://webperso.iut.univ-paris8.fr/~rosmord/nomhiero.html

BIBLIOGRAPHY

The cat in ancient Egypt

In English

author	Jaromir MALEK
publisher	British Museum Press for the Trustees of the British Museum
year	1993

Cats of Cairo

In English

author	Lorraine CHITTOCK
publisher	Camel Caravan Press – Cairo, Egypt
year	1994

The British Museum Book of cats – Ancient and Modern

In English

author	Juliet CLUTTON-BROCK
publisher	British Museum Press for the Trustees of the British Museum
year	2000

De quelle couleur seront mes chatons ?
(What colour will my kittens be ?)

in French

author	Alise BRISSON
publisher	Éditions du Point Vétérinaire
year	1989

Le chat de race
Conseils d'élevage et abrégé de génétique de la robe.

in French

author	Alise BRISSON
publisher	Chiron éditions
year	2003

Les chats mots

in French

author	Anne DUPEREY
publisher	Editions Ramsay
year	2003

Les chats de Yann Arthus-Bertrand

in French

author	Photos de Yann ARTHUS-BERTRAND Textes de Danièle LARUELLE
publisher	Chêne
year	1993

Les chatons des îles grecques

in French

auteur	Hans SILVESTER
publisher	Editions de la Martinière
year	1999

Les chats de Hans Silvester

in French

author	Hans SILVESTER
publisher	Editions de la Martinière
year	2000

Citations et proverbes chats et chiens

in French

author	Didier HALLÉPÉE
publisher	Editions Carrefour du Net
year	2009

The Reynard cycle

In ancient French

Dating from the Middle Ages
With Tybert the cat…

Les pensées du chat Mau (Mau mews)

in French and in English

author	Didier HALLÉPÉE
publisher	Carrefour du Net
year	2010 - 2011

Mon chat m'a dit (my cat told me)

in French and in English

author	Didier HALLÉPÉE
publisher	Carrefour du Net
year	2010 - 2011

Conclusion

This is the end of this book.

We have spent a very nice moment with you, sharing our passion for the Egyptian Mau.

Maybe some chapters are of interest only to fanciers. For my part, my preferred passages are those in which I talk about our own cats, these strange creatures with extraordinary personality who have chosen to put up with human beings and theircontradictions...

I will not leave the Mau world without paying a tribute to our house cats which with whom we have discovered the feline world and who have accompanied us in our discovery of the Mau: Judan, Yoda, Justin, Jackie, Juno, Kali, Mathias.

I also wish to pay tribute to Lord, our Abyssinian cat, who was our first breed cat and thanks to whom we discovered the world of cat shows and the breeding world with his fiancee, Lakmé.

Let me not forget Marvin, our wonderful Angora who, lost in a herd of Maus, still manages to capture the affection of visitors.

In short, whether Maus cats or house cats, the most important is the personal relationship we humans and cats have with each other.

SUMMARY

WELCOME TO THE MARVELLOUS WORLD OF THE EGYPTIAN MAU CAT	**9**
THE ORIGINS OF THE CAT	**10**
The main species of cats	**10**
Felis sylvestris, the European wild cat	*10*
Felis lybica, the African wild cat	*11*
Felis chaus, the jungle cat	*11*
Felis margarita, the sand cat	*12*
Felis bieti, the Chinese desert cat	*12*
Felis manul, the Pallas cat	*13*
Felis nigripes, the black-footed cat	*13*
Cat and prehistoy	**14**
The Egyptian origin	**15**
The world conquest	**23**
The Asian and the Siberian origin	**26**
The Asian origin	*26*
The Siberian origin	*27*
The blue cats origin	*27*
Conclusion about origins	*28*
FIRST MAUS STORY	**29**
Princess Troubetzkoï's Maus	**29**
Oriental Spotted Tabby	**31**
The first breeding	**32**
The Indian line	**35**
The other Egypt imports	**38**
The Mau in Europe	**42**
AIME	**44**

Presentation of AIME   **44**
   Mau protection   *44*
   Mau promotion   *45*
   Mau breeding   *46*

AIME Code of Ethic   **46**
   Skills   *46*
   Sharing information   *46*
   Legislation   *47*
   Breeding conditions   *47*
   Acquisition of maus   *47*
   Breeding   *48*
   Quality   *48*
   Prices and official documents   *48*
   Guarantees   *48*
   Early sterilization (France)   *49*
   Showing   *49*
   Deontology   *49*

AIME actions   **50**
   The database   *50*
   The fight against consanguinity   *50*
   The introduction of fresh blood   *51*
   The work on standards   *52*
   The promotion and protection of the Bronze Mau   *52*
   The recognition of the Black Mau   *53*
   The conservation of the standard   *54*
   DNA Tests   *54*
   The sharing of experience   *55*
   Shows and specials   *55*
   The Newsletter   *55*

Some figures   **57**

THE COLORS OF THE MAU   **58**

The classical ones: silver, bronze, black smoke and black   **58**
   silver   *59*
   bronze   *59*

black smoke	*60*
black	*60*

The blue — **62**

The Shirazi — **62**

Genetic elements — **63**
- Transmission of genes — *63*
- *Rules to remember* — *65*
- *Statistical rules* — *65*

Cat genetics — **66**
- *L gene: hair length* — *66*
- *Hr gene: presence of hair* — *66*
- *R gene: Cornish Rex texture* — *66*
- *Gen Re: Devon Rex texture* — *66*
- *Gene Wh: wire hair* — *66*
- *W gene: dominant white (White)* — *66*
- *B gene: Base Color* — *67*
- *C gene: color distribution* — *67*
- *Ch gene: Chinchilla* — *67*
- *Gene A: Agouti* — *67*
- *I gene: inhibition* — *67*
- *D gene: dilution* — *68*
- *Ta gene: ticking* — *68*
- *Mc gene: Coat pattern (striped or mackerel)* — *68*
- *Sp Gene: coat pattern (Spotted)* — *69*
- *S gene: White spots (white spotting)* — *69*
- *O gene: Red* — *69*

The genetics of Mau — **71**
- *Sp Gene: coat pattern (Spotted)* — *72*
- *Colors crossing* — *74*

STANDARDS — **76**

Permissible colors — **76**

Introduction — **77**

Head	77
Muzzle	77
Eyes	77
Ears	77
Neck	77
Body	78
Legs	78
Feet	78
Tail	78
Coat and texture	78
Patterns	78
Colors	79
Silver	*79*
Bronze	*79*
Black smoke	*79*
Black	*79*
Allowances	79
Penalize	80
Withhold all awards	80
Points	80
Head (30 points)	*80*
Body (30 points)	*80*
Coat and texture (40 points)	*80*
THE MAU TEMPER	82
A gluey temper	82
Very discreet	82
Expressive	82
Sometimes bashful	82

Often gluttonous	83
A speedy cat	83
A strong personality	84
SOME EGYPTIAN MAUS	85
Vasar	85
Élendril	86
Sen-sen	87
Anwar and Pharaoh	89
Sahourê	90
Khâlifa	92
Otta	93
Maslama	94
Élinor	95
Fleur	96
Kiyasa	98
Pakhet	99
Nout	99
Dot's Heart	101
Renen	102
Sarina	103
Resout	104
Marie-Chantal	105
Senefer	106
Senet	107
Tiw & Tep-Nefer	109
Bronzie	111

Sothis	**111**
Swnet	**112**
Uther Pendragon	**113**
Velleda	**115**
EGYPTIAN NAMES FOR EGYPTIANS CATS	**116**
Beginning with B	*116*
1999 – names beginning with P	*117*
2000 – names beginning with R	*118*
2001 – names beginning with S	*120*
2003 – names beginning with U	*124*
LES STARS DE L'AIME	**125**
1998	**125**
CE VASAR	*125*
GC, BW, RW Brockhaven OSIRA	*126*
GC, RW Brockhaven MAFDET	*126*
DM Brockhaven PHILOMENE	*126*
1999	**127**
CE ELENDRIL du Nil Blanc	*127*
GC Brockhaven KALAKALA	*127*
2000	**128**
SAHOURÊ of Fondcombe	*128*
2001	**128**
GC, RW Brockhaven SEN-SEN of Fondcombe	*128*
GC Tavaron's DOTTE COOLPEPPER	*129*
2002	**129**
CHI SENEFER de Fondcombe	*129*
CE, GC, RW Brockhaven SEN-SEN of Fondcombe	*130*
GCE IMHOTEP RA-LAIDACH della Dea Sekhmet	*130*
CH Imhotep SOBEK	*131*
GCE Princesse NEFERMEREN de Fondcombe	*131*
2003	**132**
GCE, GC, RW Brockhaven SEN-SEN of Fondcombe	*132*

CH TWT de Fondcombe	132
Imhotep TRIPHAENA CLEOPÂTRA	133

2004   133

GCE SENEKKW de Bélénus	133
UTHER PENDRAGON de Fondcombe	134
UPSWING et UPPER-EGYPT de Fondcombe	134
GC Tavaron's DOTTE COOLPEPPER	135

THE SPECIAL MAU SHOWS IN FRANCE   136

Chinagora show 2001   137

Attending cats - Silver	137
Attending cats - Black Smoke	138
Attending cats - Bronze	138
October 13	138
October 14: Short hair:	139

Special Mau, Chinagora 2002   140

Attending cats - Silver	140
Attending cats - Black Smoke	142
Attending cats - Bronze	142
Results of the special (26/10/02)	143

Special Mau, Aubevoye 2003   144

Attending cats - Silver	144
Attending cats - Black Smoke	145
Attending cats - Bronze	146
The best on 19/04/2003)	146
The best on 20/04/2003)	146
Results of the special (20/04/2003)	147

Special, Chinagora 2003   148

Attending cats - Silver	148
Attending cats - Black Smoke	149
Attending cats - Bronze	149
Attending cat – Black	150
Results of saturday 29/11/03	150
Results of sunday 30/11/03	151

Special, Antony 2004	**152**
Attending cats - Silver	152
Attending cats - Black Smoke	153
Attending cats - Bronze	153
Results of saturday 07/02/2004	154
Results of sunday 08/02/2004	154
Special, Sannois 2006	**156**
Attending cats - Silver	156
Attending cats - Black Smoke	156
Attending cats - Bronze	157
Results of saturday 11/02/2006	157
Results of sunday 12/02/2006	157
Special, Poissy 2007	**159**
Attending cats - Silver	159
Attending cats - Black Smoke	161
Attending cats - Bronze	161
Results of Sunday 07/10/2007	162
Special, Monaco 2011	**163**
Attending cats – Silver	163
Attending cats - Black Smoke	164
Attending cats - Bronze	164
Attending cats - Black	164
Results of sunday 30/01/2011	165
EUROPEAN CHAMPIONS AND GRAND CHAMPIONS	**166**
CE VASAR	166
CE ELENDRIL du Nil Blanc	166
GCE IMHOTEP RA-LAIDACH della Dea Sekhmet	167
GCE, GC, RW Brockhaven SEN-SEN of Fondcombe	167
GCE Princesse NEFERMEREN de Fondcombe	168
GCE SENEKKW de Bélénus	168
GCE, CH (CFA) Tavaron's SARINA of Fondcombe	169
CE SENET de Fondcombe	169
CE Imhotep SOBEK	170
THE MAU AT HOME	**171**

Choosing a kitten	*171*
Formalities	*172*
Arriving at home	**173**
May the cat go out?	**174**
Some health suggestions	**175**
Grooming	*175*
Eyes	*175*
Ears	*175*
Claws	*175*
Hair	*175*
Bath	*176*
Litter	*176*
If it pees everywhere?	*177*
Food	*177*
Affection	*178*
Diarrhoeas	*178*
Fevers, colds, etc	*178*
QUOTATIONS ABOUT CATS	**180**
Inscription on the Royal Tombs at Thebes	**180**
Anonymous quotations	**180**
Quotations by author	**184**
THE EGYPTIAN MAU ON THE WEB	**222**
Cats and Egypt	**222**
Cats and Egypt	*222*
The Egyptian Mau clubs	**222**
Association Internationale du Mau Egyptien (AIME)	*222*
Egyptian Mau Breeders' and Fanciers' Club (EMBFC)	*222*
The Egyptian Mau Club	*222*
Global Egyptian Mau Society (GEMS)	*223*
Egyptian Mau Enthusiasts (EME)	*223*
The author's web site	**223**
Fondcombe Cattery	*223*

The Egyptian Mau Forum	**223**
Maus d'Amour, the forum	223
The Cat associations	**223**
European Cat Fancy	223
Federazione Italiana Associazione Feline (FIAF)	223
Feline Fancier of Belgium	223
Cat Friends of Germany e. V (CFG)	224
Cat Fancier Association (CFA)	224
American Cat Fancier Association (ACFA)	224
The International Cat Association (TICA)	224
American Association of Cat Enthusiasts (AACE)	224
Katz Incorporated – New Zealand (KATZ)	224
The e-groups	**224**
EmauC	224
EMBFC	224
MauCats	225
Mau-of-Egypt	225
G-E-M-S	225
maugang	225
egyptianmaus	225
rizykitty	225
Miscellaneous	**226**
Dr Susan Little's website	226
Gianfranco Montovani home page	226
Bastet	226
Glossaire félin	226
Egyptian Name translator	226
Nom en hiéroglyphes	227
BIBLIOGRAPHY	**228**
The cat in ancient Egypt	228
Cats of Cairo	228
The British Museum Book of cats – Ancient and Modern	228
De quelle couleur seront mes chatons ?	228
Le chat de race	229

Les chats mots	*229*
Les chats de Yann Arthus-Bertrand	*229*
Les chatons des îles grecques	*229*
Les chats de Hans Silvester	*229*
Citations et proverbes chats et chiens	*230*
The Reynard cycle	*230*
Les pensées du chat Mau (Mau mews)	*230*
Mon chat m'a dit (my cat told me)	*230*
CONCLUSION	**232**

Extracts from: **Mot à mau – Mau Mews**

PROVERBE AFRICAIN – PROVERB FROM AFRICA

The one who heard of the tiger and the one who saw the tiger don't run the same way.

PROVERBE CHINOIS – PROVERB FROM CHINA

It is difficult to catch a black cat in a dark room. Especially when he is not there.

CITATION – QUOTATION: RICARDO PHILIPS

You can not have better life than cats: they do what they want when they want, all they want.

CITATION – QUOTATION: THÉOPHILE GAUTIER

The man complains to live! Does he not have hands to stroke the fur of cats!

Read our illustrated quotations in:

Mot à mau – Mau Mews
Didier Hallépée
Publisher: Carrefour du Net

Bilingual edition

MOT À MAU
LES PENSÉES DU CHAT MAU

Come, superb cat, on my amorous heart — **DIDIER HALLÉPÉE**

COLLECTION ARC-EN-CIEL
ANIMAUX

Around 4000 years ago, the Egyptians invented the grain silo. The silos have attracted rodents then snakes then cats. This was the beginning of the great adventure of the domestic cat.

At the heart of this adventure, the Egyptian Mau, true descendant of Pharaoh cats, holds the first place. This is his story that we contons today.

Only naturally spotted cat, it exists in 4 colors: silver, bronze, black smoke and solid black. Her eyes are gooseberry green and in the depths of his enigmatic gaze, 40 centuries of feline friendship look down on you.

His temper full of personality makes him the typical feline. Demigod himself, he seduced Pharaoh. Certainly, it will seduce you also.

Graduate of Polytechnic (Paris), PhD of Mathematics, Phd of Computer Sciences, **Didier HALLÉPÉE** is also cat breeder (Fondcombe cattery).

Fallen in love of the Egyptian Mau, he shared his passion of the mau through the AIME, the International Association for Egyptian Mau.